Praise for **The Purpose of Purpose**

"Rare is the business book that will have you throw your head back with laughter yet constantly set you straight with the truth. This is that uncommon and exceptional work."
SCOTT MCKAIN, bestselling author of *ICONIC*

"This book reconnects the importance of growth with the power of purpose in a way that is unique, hilarious, practical, and profound."
MICHAEL BUNGAY STANIER, bestselling author of *The Coaching Habit*

"This book is like a TED Talk for the caffeinated and slightly jaded. It's equal parts thought-provoking and laugh-out-loud funny, packed with stories that make you think."
ROBERT ROSE, author of *Content Marketing Strategy*

"While the rest of the business world sits around a conference table and eats free muffins and talks brand and strategy and blah blah blah... only Ron Tite asks the bigger questions: 'What's the purpose of our brand, anyway? And why does it matter to you, me, and our customers?'"
TINA FEY (aka Ann Handley, bestselling author of *Everybody Writes*)

"Ron Tite brilliantly redefines what it means to lead with purpose in a world that demands it. This isn't about lofty ideals or empty slogans. It's a clear, actionable road map for leaders looking to drive real impact."
MICHELE ROMANOW, *Dragons' Den* investor

"Ron Tite shows how the best in the world combine purpose and growth to achieve phenomenal results. This book will help you turn marketing speak into leadership action."
JOEY COLEMAN, bestselling author of *Never Lose an Employee Again*

"With his signature blend of humor, wisdom, and razor-sharp insights, Ron Tite brilliantly dismantles outdated notions of purpose and replaces them with a transformative framework that ties meaningful growth to actionable beliefs."
MICHAEL PORT, bestselling author of *Steal the Show*

"This book doesn't offer a bunch of hollow ideas—it hands you the tools to climb on your own."
ALISON LEVINE, bestselling author of *On the Edge*

"Ron Tite gets it. Business, strategy, culture, growth... the whole shebang. This volume is packed with the stories, frameworks, and tactics to help you make purpose the fuel for your organization's growth."
LIANE DAVEY, bestselling author of *The Good Fight*

"If strategy is the map, purpose is your compass. This book ensures you and your team are never lost."
STEPHEN SHAPIRO, author of *PIVOTAL*

"A rallying cry for leaders to stop performative purpose and corporate virtue signaling, and instead use purpose to focus decisions, create meaningful experiences, and develop extraordinary organizations."
SHAWN KANUNGO, bestselling author of *The Bold Ones*

THE PURPOSE OF PURPOSE

Ron Tite

THE PURPOSE

**Making growth
the heart of
your business**

OF PURPOSE

- PAGE
- TWO

Copyright © 2025 by Ron Tite

All rights reserved. No part of this book may be reproduced, stored in a retrieval system or transmitted, in any form or by any means, without the prior written consent of the publisher or a license from The Canadian Copyright Licensing Agency (Access Copyright). For a copyright license, visit accesscopyright.ca or call toll free to 1-800-893-5777.

Some names and identifying details have been changed to protect the privacy of individuals.

Cataloguing in publication information is available from Library and Archives Canada.
ISBN 978-1-77458-580-1 (hardcover)
ISBN 978-1-77458-634-1 (ebook)

Page Two
pagetwo.com

PAGE TWO™ is a trademark owned by Page Two Strategies Inc., and is used under license by authorized licensees

Cover design by Peter Cocking
Interior design by Taysia Louie
Printed and bound in Canada by Friesens
Distributed in Canada by Raincoast Books
Distributed in the US and internationally by Macmillan

25 26 27 28 29   5 4 3 2 1

thinkdosay.com

To Christy, Max, and Benny

A book that someone actually wrote?!

What a joy!

Everyone else is just using ChatGPT.

PLATO

Contents

Foreword by Mitch Joel *1*
I Hate Introductions *7*

1. **Be like Bo** *9*
2. **It's the End of the World as We Know It (and I Don't Feel Fine)** *27*
3. **Now What? Growth's What** *51*
4. **Think, Do, Say, Grow** *85*
5. **Focused by Purpose (The THINK Part)** *113*
6. **Defined by Your Actions (The DO Part)** *149*
   a. **The Personalized Experience** *171*
   b. **The Frictionless Experience** *191*
   c. **The Employee Experience** *211*
7. **Adopted through Communications (The SAY Part)** *233*
8. **Go Forth and Multiply** *275*

Acknowledgments *291*
References *295*

Foreword

WHAT IS the purpose of life?
...
...
Umm...
...to procreate?
...to be a "good person"?
...to add value to this world?
Umm...
What is the purpose of work?
...
...
Umm...
...to make enough money to survive and provide for my family (and myself)?
...to personally develop and learn life lessons in and around the areas of responsibility, pride, determination, self-satisfaction, and problem-solving?
...to pursue some kind of "meaning" for my life?
...to align more closely with others who have shared values?
...to provide a sense of personal accomplishment?

None of these answers seem to satiate the question.

Most of these answers seem to open up much deeper and self-reflective questions.

These self-reflective questions may not produce the answers we want to hear.

So... again... what is the purpose of work? (Which is a question worth exploring, considering the vast majority of us spend the bulk of our waking hours toiling away at it... and when we're not working, we're often thinking about it, talking about it to our family and friends, or thumbing through our inbox/to-do lists.)

We have unprecedented levels of automation (and more to come with artificial intelligence and robotics) for the work that we do, and sadly, we are not working any fewer hours than those who worked before us (which doesn't make any sense).

How can we have this much automation and computational power and yet we're still working more hours (and are more stressed) than our ancestors?

So... if we're going to be working like this, our work should have purpose.

The business that we work for should have purpose.

Fair?

Well... maybe?

Because we can also "work" on things beyond our job...

We can work on our physical health (try that Ganja Yoga class... it's a thing... google it), our mental health (post your Headspace streak below!), our relationships (when was the last time you called your mother?!?), or the stuff that gives us joy (that LEGO *Harry Potter* Hogwarts Castle isn't going to build itself!).

Now, if that is true, then we (mostly) work to make money?

In 2021, James Suzman authored *Work: A Deep History, from the Stone Age to the Age of Robots*. Think of it as a history of humankind through the lens of work (what it is... why we do it... and why it so deeply defines us). From the book:

> When economists define work as time and effort we spend meeting our needs and wants, they dodge two obvious problems. The first is that often the only thing that differentiates work from leisure is context and whether we are being paid to do something or are paying to do it... The closest thing to a universal definition of "work"—one that hunter-gatherers, pinstriped derivatives traders, calloused subsistence farmers, and anyone else would agree on—is that it involves purposefully expending energy or effort on a task to achieve a goal or end.

There's that "purpose" word again.

Now let's layer on some speed to the equation.

"Business is moving at the speed of light." "Things are moving faster and faster." "It's hard to keep up with how fast things are moving."

When was the pace of work not fast?

When was technology not pushing us to work faster?

Isn't all of this constant talk about speed... exhausting?

So, if everyone keeps saying that the purpose of our work is to be faster than the competition or to keep pace with the industry, there can't be much purpose in it (unless every business that sells anything has the same purpose).

Brazilian author and beloved human Paulo Coelho wrote: "Change. But start slowly, because direction is more important than speed."

Where you're going (and the thoughtfulness around this decision) is more important than how quickly we move.

Why you're going in that direction (and how you will grow on the journey) is the purpose of defining your purpose.

How do we know?

A famed tech company has pushed its purpose of helping local businesses build vibrant and diverse communities and takes pride in how many LGBTQ2S+ employees and clients they serve. It's admirable, and it is a sincere part of their purpose.

Still, tell that to the people in the 200 jobs they just cut as part of a "strategic reorganization aimed at focusing on profitable growth." (No mention of diversity or purpose in that press release.)

Patagonia is a billion-dollar sustainable clothing brand with close to 100 stores worldwide. Its purpose could not be clearer or more admired. (Check out the 2005 book by Yvon Chouinard, the company's founder, *Let My People Go Surfing*.)

Recently, the business has let its people go surfing indefinitely via layoffs, and many team members are accusing the company of losing its soul and prioritizing profits over sustainability (you know, their purpose).

The purpose of purpose is found in your direction and your growth along the way.

That purpose might need to shine even brighter when things are dark. (Like reputation, it can take years to build and one instant to destroy.)

Never forget that.

Purpose is more than what the brand stands for.

Purpose is more than making it come alive in an ad campaign.

Purpose is more than the values written on the company's website or reception walls.

Purpose is the reason we get up in the morning.

Purpose is the reason we do it again the following day.

Purpose is the reason consumers spend their money, time, and attention on you (and not your competitors).

You can't fake purpose. (Well, you can, but you really shouldn't.)

And, yes, there is a purpose to having purpose.

Turn the page and Ron will show you what it is, how to uncover it, and—most importantly—how to live it.

MITCH JOEL
Founder of ThinkersOne and author of
Six Pixels of Separation and *Ctrl Alt Delete*
Montreal, December 2024

I Hate Introductions

IF YOU want an introduction, I suggest going to eHarmony, Bumble, or an old-school matchmaker. They can make introductions to people through a series of dinners and coffee dates that will leave you wondering how humanity gets anything done.

This is a book.
I'm not here to introduce you to the topic.
I'm here to explore it.
So booooooo to introductions.

Start your engines.
I certainly started mine.

"Don't talk to me about my personal brand, and I won't talk to you about your why. Just as long as both of us can talk about CrossFit."

ABRAHAM LINCOLN

BE
LIKE
BO

You may not know who Bo Burnham is. But you should.

Make Happier

There's a groundbreaking video on YouTube that, on the surface, doesn't really look groundbreaking at all.

It starts with a 16-year-old boy stepping into frame, looking at the camera, and saying, "Hi, gang. I just woke up, and I thought I'd serenade you with a song. It's about my life and it's something I need to come to realize and all of you should come to realize... Take it as it is, digest it, soak it in, then use it as you will."

He proceeds to play piano and sing the type of song one would expect from a 16-year-old. Nothing special, right?

His name is Bo Burnham.

And that is the first video he ever uploaded to YouTube.

You may not know who Bo Burnham is. But you should. I think he's one of the most important artists of our time. Not just for his art but for his career, too.

Bo began innocently enough as a kid exploring self-expression with new tools of production and distribution from the comfort of his teenaged-angst-filled bedroom. He didn't have Farrah Fawcett or Ken Dryden posters on his walls like I did. He had a Casio keyboard, a digital video camera, and Wi-Fi.

Over time, Bo composed, performed, recorded, and uploaded humorous songs to YouTube. People loved it. His popularity grew, his subscriptions increased, and views and likes rolled in.

Right on cue, that's when the haters came out. I'm embarrassed to admit that I was one of them. When people called him a comedian, I strenuously objected.

I spent 20 years in stand-up slugging it out onstage. I had experienced soul-destroying moments when the only sound that followed my punch line was a muffled cough from the back of the room. Those moments of failure didn't destroy me. They defined me.

Comedians didn't perform alone in their bedrooms. They stood on a stage behind a microphone and in front of real people making jokes about airplanes and the differences between men and women. Didn't they?

When Bo appeared on Paul Provenza's show *The Green Room*, he said this of his critics:

> The biggest reason people gave me shit is because I came out of the internet, they said I didn't get enough criticism—I wasn't in the clubs grinding it out. But the truth is, for the older comics to say that, I want them to read 10,000 internet comments and see if they don't feel fully criticized... The first comment I ever got when I was 15 was "Go Go Gadget Faggot."

Me trying to define comedy with my tightly focused definition is like thinking taxis are the only way for people to get around, buying in-store is the only definition of commerce, and portable music is defined as an album you carry around with you.

I was wrong. And I hate that I thought that. But I did. And I wasn't the only one.

Hell, maybe Bo thought it, too.

Before long, he bowed to the pressure, left his room, and ventured out into the world to do live shows.

By 2015, Bo was regularly touring the country, and in 2016, Netflix picked up his show *Make Happy*. I still remember the first time I saw it. I was at home thinking, "Oh, this will be fun. A show called *Make Happy* will probably make me happy."

Then I watched it. Gulp.

I wasn't happy. I was sad.
I was angry.
I was depressed.
I was confused. I was curious.
I was engaged.
I was stumped.
I was torn.

At the end of that show, I was a bunch of things, but happy wasn't at the top of the list. More than anything, his performance really made me think.

In Bo's second last song, "Can't Handle This" (a brilliant number inspired by Kanye West), he looked out to his audience—his paying clients—and admitted that his biggest problem in life was them. Sure, one part of him loved them. But another part HATED them. While he needed them, he also feared them. He sung about knowing full well that they were there to get something from from him that sadly, he couldn't give himself.

He dropped the mic, left the stage, and went to a different room to sing one last quick song alone. Then he got up from the piano, walked out the door, and quit doing stand-up comedy.

Gulp.

Walking away from the company you work for may have come to life for many of you in the pandemic, but for Bo, it started here.

As he would later explain on the podcast *Good One*, he quit because of panic attacks. He was an accomplished performer who couldn't perform in front of people. As he described it, "It's like a chef who's starving."

That second last song wasn't just called "Can't Handle This." He literally couldn't handle it.

Boy, talk about an inspiring way to start this book, huh? You showed up for humor and insight, and I kick it off with a depressing career case study that has you reaching for a Percocet while you update your LinkedIn profile. I'm telling you to emulate *this guy's* career?

Well, yeah. Stay with me. Because a few years after *Make Happy*, the pandemic happened, and Bo went back to that room.

He returned to the location where he had left his work to reinvent his work. Forced to perform in an audience-free environment, he enthusiastically embraced his limitations and created the show *Inside*.

By create, I mean he composed it.
He played it.
He sang it.
He shot it.
He lit it.
He cut it.
He mixed it.

Inside is absolutely brilliant, and I think it's his finest work to date. He combined music, comedy, and social commentary to explore politics, technology, and mental health. He experimented with new formats, new technology, and new genres. He combined what he knew with what he didn't. He connected his original purpose with what he wanted to explore.

Bo was nominated for six Emmys for *Inside*. He won three of them: for writing, directing, and music direction—awards rarely won by the same person.

While the rest of the world was stopping, Bo was starting.

While the rest of the world was complaining,
Bo was exploring.

While the rest of the world was meeting, Bo was moving.

While the rest of the world was quitting, Bo was creating.

While the rest of the world was stuck, Bo was in motion.

While the rest of the world was provoking responses,
Bo was provoking thought.

While the rest of us were simply trying to survive,
Bo embraced his limitations, revisited what first brought him joy, and used the opportunity to completely reinvent himself and his work.

While the rest of the world was searching for purpose,
Bo reconnected with his.

While the rest
of the world
was quitting,
Bo was creating.

Do It like the Jerk

The reinvention that Bo initiated has always captured my attention.

In my first book, *Everyone's an Artist (or at Least They Should Be)*, I wrote of my admiration for Steve Martin. Look, I love where I'm at in life, but if I had to swap careers with anyone else in the world, I'd pick Steve Martin (except he'd say, "No way, Mr. ... Mr. ... Is it pronounced 'Teetay'?").

He may have taught a MasterClass on comedy, but he should really teach one on career management. His relentless pursuit of personal growth has pushed him to stints as a writer, stand-up comedian, actor, playwright, and musician, much of it with great success. He's won an honorary Oscar, five Grammys (Grammies?), an Emmy, the Mark Twain Prize, and the Kennedy Center Honors. I'm sure he has a few Scouts badges in there, too.

My friend Preet Banerjee and I went to see "An Evening with Steve Martin" in Toronto, and host Rick Mercer included this tidbit in his opening: "In the early '70s, only three nonathletic events sold out Toronto's Maple Leaf Gardens: the Beatles, Elvis Presley, and Steve Martin."

He quit his writing gig on *The Smothers Brothers Comedy Hour* to do stand-up. Near the peak of his success, he abruptly quit stand-up to act and starred in *Roxanne, Parenthood, ¡Three Amigos!, L.A. Story, Father of the Bride*, and many others. He authored the bestselling novella *Shopgirl* and wrote one of my favorite memoirs, *Born Standing Up*. He has written several plays, including *Picasso at the Lapin Agile* and *Meteor Shower*. He has released several bluegrass albums, including *The Crow: New Songs for the Five-String Banjo*.

Like Bo Burnham, he embraced the limitations of the COVID-19 pandemic and collaborated with *New Yorker* cartoonist Harry Bliss to create *A Wealth of Pigeons*, a collection of more than 130 cartoons. An avid art collector, he was also the lead curator of a Lawren Harris exhibit that toured North America. In 2020, he teamed up with John Hoffman to create *Only Murders in the Building* and invited old friend Martin Short and new friend Selena Gomez to join him.

While other men his age are yelling at people to get off their lawns, Steve Martin is reimagining what the lawn is and inviting them on to help him make it better.

Steve's ability (Can I just call him Steve?) to reinvent himself and succeed in various fields is a testament to his versatility, creativity, and unwavering dedication to personal development—never content with where he is and always exploring where he can go.

Bound by purpose.
Defined by the actions he takes.
And his ideas, passions, and "products" are adopted by others through his unique communication and continuity and consistency of brand.

From Steve, who has done it all, to Bo, who seems to want to experience it all, these artists provide a valuable lesson to the rest of us:

The only thing worse than the Great Resignation is the Great Resignation.

Resignation Recall

Normally, when we speak of the "Great Resignation," we mean the phenomenon that emerged during the "global event that won't be named" when a significant number of workers quit their jobs.

People questioned every aspect of their very existence, not to mention their employment. Some experienced burnout, some reflected on their career goals, and some looked to the sky and asked, "What the hell does all this mean??!"

The result?

A whack of people looked around their workplace and thought, "This sucks. I quit. I'm outta here."

The Great Resignation.

It was a reaction to a seemingly unfavorable situation. Millions left their jobs in search of greener pastures, richer comp, and better dental. It was like some corporate version of musical chairs where an underpaid DJ stopped the music, forcing everyone to stumble around in search of a new chair—in this case, a cushier one than before. We had a writer who worked for us during the pandemic, and she came to me and said, "I have an offer from another agency." She told me the compensation they promised and asked, "What should I do?" My response? "You should be calling me from your new desk. Take the cash."

The pandemic continues to affect the job market in post-pandemic times, and it remains to be seen whether the Great Resignation will continue, subside, or whether it created a new normal. Regardless, it highlighted the importance of work-life balance, reprioritized employee well-being, and it finally forced businesses to address injustices and inequalities and forced us to discuss how work impacts mental health.

All in all, it was a good thing. But it's not the only thing. I don't even think it's the most important thing. There's another version of the Great Resignation, because there's another definition of "resignation."

The only thing worse than the Great Resignation is the Great Resignation.

When someone is merely resigned.

They're resigned to doing what they've always done.

They're resigned to just going about their day the way they've always gone about their day.

They're resigned to making the same decisions, following the same processes, having the same conversations with the same people, leading to the same outcomes.

They're resigned to limiting their behaviors to their current job title.

They're resigned to meeting expectations, not surpassing them.

They're resigned to being the person that stuff happens to instead of being the person that makes stuff happen.

They're resigned to choosing apathy over action.

They're resigned to their fate.

They're resigned to existing without a purpose.

So no, it's not a reaction to an unfavorable situation. It's worse.

It's an acceptance of one. *This* Great Resignation is way worse for your business, it's way worse for your career, and it's way worse for your mental health. And no one's talking about it.

This Great Resignation is the one we should really be focused on because all the things that the original

Great Resignation is meant to improve will never happen if individuals are resigned to accepting them.

We have an amazing opportunity before us and our organizations—all of us—to have our Bo Burnham moment. It's not about going backward to recovery. It's about going forward to reinvention. We can reconnect with our purpose, create new and interesting actions that drive progress, and evolve into new versions of ourselves.

Why? Is this just rearranging the furniture in the living room because you're a little bored with the setup? Is this about launching a new division because you're tired of the business you're in? Is this pivoting to an entirely new model because you feel peer pressure to use the word "pivot" in a LinkedIn post?

No. It's because business has significantly changed since the pandemic and will change with greater velocity over the next two years. And when there's a seismic shift, what usually follows is clarity, creation, and carnage. I don't know about you, but carnage isn't something I want to sign up for.

Let me be frank. In many cases, I think big business has failed you.

It failed us, too. All of us.

When the world around it was hinting at change, big business didn't budge. When the world demanded change, it took the easy way out. It pretended to care, checked a bunch of boxes, and not only did it do a disservice to our communities, it also did a complete disservice to itself.

Business didn't just get the very idea of purpose wrong. Business got drunk on ideals, got high on values, and totally sloshed on a version of purpose that had nothing to do with how they made their money or how they spent their time.

The version of corporate purpose that most people applaud and promote is just wrong.

How did we get it so wrong?
Don't worry. I gotchu. I'll tell you all about it.
Let's go. Let's grow.

"Let's be honest, fam.

If you're not trending, you're pretending."

JULIUS CAESAR

IT'S THE END OF THE WORLD AS WE KNOW IT
(AND I DON'T FEEL FINE)

Let's face it,
Extra Gum
got it wrong.

It's Time

Extra Gum celebrated the end of the pandemic with an epic spot called "For When It's Time." It hit all the feels.

The spot opens with scenes of deserted streets and empty offices with an onscreen message that simply states, "Sometime in the not-too-distant future."

As one guy wakes from hibernation, a radio DJ excitedly announces, "This just in. We are back! We can see people again!"

With that flip of the isolation switch, people start physically emerging from their homes and mentally emerging from their *Tiger King*–induced cobwebs.

They shut down Zoom.
They put on clothes.
They greet their neighbors.
They gather in parks and make out with strangers.
Who didn't? It was a gum commercial.
What did you expect?

All the "We're free" vignettes are perfectly accompanied by Céline Dion's "It's All Coming Back to Me Now."

Even now, the spot is surprisingly moving—and triggering. I weep tears of joy, I panic from stress, and I beat my chest in fist-bumping rhythm just as Céline would.

Still, the spot isn't exactly how the end of the pandemic went down.

It was how we *thought* it would end.

Many of us believed that someone from the World Health Organization would call a press conference, step up to a microphone, and cheerfully announce, "It's over!" and then we'd return to our regularly scheduled programming. Well, no switch was flipped. Instead, it was a dimmer that kept turning left and right with stops and starts and half-baked promises followed by apologies, warnings, and new variants that would appear like the Great Gazoo.

To this day, I still don't think we've ever actually celebrated the end of the pandemic, have we?

Let's face it, Extra Gum got it wrong. And they really got the last few seconds of the spot wrong. In its final moments, people grabbed their briefcases, enthusiastically put on business-appropriate clothing, and ran through the streets before forcing their way into their office buildings, where they hugged and reunited with the colleagues they so desperately missed.

Extra actually thought that everyone would sprint back to the office to hug their bosses and colleagues? As we say in Canada, "Yeah, no..."

That didn't happen. In fact, the exact opposite did.

People fought return-to-office mandates and attempted to reinvent the very nature of work. They didn't just complain about senior management around the virtual watercooler. They used years of perceived and real inequality, which had come to a head during the pandemic, to redefine what work meant, how it was completed, and how it was run.

It wasn't the pandemic specifically that gave them fuel for the fire; it was all the stuff that happened during the pandemic—from government handouts and trucker gatherings to George Floyd, expanding definitions of gender, TikTok trends, and early appearances of AI. While some businesses were fighting for survival, business-bashing from the front lines was the hottest ticket in town.

But the bashing didn't start in the pandemic, and it certainly didn't end when it was over.

Flipping the Bird to Biz

You might not know it from my last name, but I'm part Italian. For the full experience, imagine me telling you this with overly animated hand gestures.

In his teens, my grandfather left the tiny town of San Nicandro in Italy's Foggia province and ventured to Montreal. Clearly, he wanted to swap fresh tomatoes and basil for cheese curds and gravy. Who wouldn't?

Sadly, I haven't been to San Nicandro. But I have been to Milan.

Right outside the Italian stock exchange in Milan's Piazza Affari, there's a big piece of marble that's kind of hard to ignore. It's not a statue of a politician, a historical or religious figure, or even an abstract shape.

It's just this big human hand.

But the hand isn't pointing, giving a hearty thumbs-up, or even doing that well-known Italian pinched-finger gesture that normally completes the phrase "Whadda you talkin' about?!"

It's flipping the bird. Giving the finger.

It's not a traditional flip, either. The hand isn't positioned to isolate the middle finger. It's the only finger left. Every other finger is cut off, leaving the middle finger alone, pointing to the sky in a defiant salute.

The message is very clear: "Fuck you."

There's just one problem. No one's sure if the Italian public is giving the finger to business or if it's business who is flipping off everyone else.

The statue, dubbed L.O.V.E., which stands for libertà (freedom), odio (hatred), vendetta (vengeance), and eternità (eternity), was crafted by Maurizio Cattelan in 2010. It was supposed to be a temporary exhibit, but the city found it a bit too potent and poignant to remove.

I'm not going to try to peer into the soul of an artist and reveal to you the true meaning of his expression. It could be a scathing critique of the economic turmoil that swept around the globe in 2008 or the role industry has played in destroying the environment.

The important part isn't about his specific grievance. It's that he's not alone. Around the globe, the hate-on for business has never been stronger.

The working class has always complained about the rich, middle management has always had a dislike for senior management, and stock exchanges have usually been seen as places where people exchange money for even more money without more work.

It just feels different now. It seems to have gone from "Business is kinda evil" to "Capitalism just doesn't work anymore, and we're bitter as hell because of it."

As the clock ticks toward our next environmental catastrophe.

As more social injustices are illuminated.

As CEO compensation continues to distance leaders from the comp of their teams.

As start-ups make their founders millions before ever turning a profit.

As fewer people can afford homes.

As billionaires avoid paying taxes so they can go to space.

As younger generations establish new working norms and put cause before compensation, it's clear that it's not just Maurizio Cattelan who's saying "fuck you" to business.

The middle finger is up. And it's not coming down anytime soon.

There Are No Dogs in Pity City

That middle finger in Milan isn't aimed only at the stock exchange; it's pointed at every leader who's forgotten what it truly means to lead. It's because of their actions that it's no surprise that Johnny Citizen has turned against them.

The middle finger is up. And it's not coming down anytime soon.

Leaders aren't just failing to adapt to the world around them. Some are actively engaged in behaviors that should be taught in the MBA class called "How Not to Lead."

In a misguided attempt to motivate her team, the CEO of MillerKnoll, Andi Owen, famously ranted at employees to "Leave pity city." What she should have said was "You want empathy? Not here. We'd prefer to illustrate just how disconnected some leaders are from the realities of their employees' lives."

Clearlink CEO James Clarke actually celebrated an employee for selling their dog. They had to do it so they could return to the office. He valued personal sacrifice to an inhumane degree, placing the company's needs above the fundamental well-being of its employees (not to mention the dog).

On one hand, mental health and well-being are finally being recognized as critical components of workplace culture. On the other, some leaders are showing themselves as out-of-touch autocrats who are more concerned with the bottom line than the human beings driving it.

Uber's former CEO, Travis Kalanick, delivered riders, food, toxic leadership, and a bad workplace environment. Activision Blizzard's Bobby Kotick overlooked sexual misconduct. Better.com's Vishal Garg fired 900 people on a Zoom call and called his employees "dumb dolphins." Boeing's David Calhoun put financial concerns ahead of safety concerns. "Pharma Bro" Martin Shkreli raised the price of Daraprim by over 5,000 percent. And do I even want to mention Elon Musk, where X marks the spot... of multiple disasters?

Employees, consumers, partners, and communities are demanding more from those who occupy the C-suite. They want leaders who are empathetic, ethical, and evolving. Leaders who understand that treating people with respect and dignity isn't just good for morale; it's good for business.

And they hope we will get these good leaders—and leave the shitty ones behind—when we reinvent capitalism. Sure, these CEOs are seen as villains, but the (slightly misguided) perception is that it's the system, not the individuals, to blame: What we need is a new capitalism—one that values long-term impact and ethical considerations over short-term gains.

As people demanded answers, the finger-pointing began, and it wasn't just coming from the public. It was coming from the Pontiff.

Praise Be

Pope Francis took to Twitter in October 2021 to issue a powerful indictment of the business world's role in aiding and abetting global crises.

From beneath his flowing, holy-water-soaked robe, he gave a stern finger-shake at senior executives in pretty much every industry.

His Holiness's call was both urgent and sweeping. He asked telecommunication companies to liberalize access to educational material. He asked tech giants to stop preying on people's weaknesses. He asked food companies to stop imposing monopolistic production and distribution. He asked real estate and agriculture businesses to stop destroying nature, financial firms to waive debt, and Big Pharma to liberalize patents. Essentially, the Pope said:

Give away the vaccines.
Cancel debts.
Stop polluting.
Stop withholding bread from the hungry.
Stop making arms.
Stop exploiting human weakness.
Give access to education.

Stop misinformation.
Stop aggression.

He ended by saying, "This system, with its relentless logic of profit, is escaping all human control."

While he has never been known for his entrepreneurial attitudes, Pope Francis was acting like an activist investor chirping from the sidelines. Even free-enterprise champions like me were left saying, "Well, he's not wronnnnnng..." even though we knew that it was a tad more complicated, and it would take more than a couple of Hail Marys to right the wrongs.

But it wasn't just the Pope.

US Green Party candidate Jason Call tweeted (X'ed??) the most bang-on criticism of pandemic public policy that was focused on saving businesses: "If capitalism is so great, why does it need to be bailed out by socialism every ten years?"

Calls were coming from the inside, too. Max Koeune, president and CEO of McCain Foods, admitted, "I think there's a growing distrust that the interests of business aren't necessarily aligned with the interests of society."

The Pope was upset, the public was upset, and executives were upset.

We saw environmental impact. Economic inequality. Labor exploitation. Corporate greed. Political influence.

Chronic waste. And technological disruption and consolidation that left Mark Zuckerberg with more influence than most elected officials.

I can hear you all thinking, "Well, when you put it that waaaaaay..."

As consumers dug deeper, they wondered if inequality wasn't just created by evil billionaires who clearly needed to revisit their purpose. Maybe it was created by the system. And if it was the system, the system would have to respond.

Our Currency Isn't Current

Back in 1988 when I was an 18-year-old, Spike Lee—through his fictional Mars Blackmon character—introduced me to Michael Jordan in a series of Nike commercials that featured the iconic line "It's gotta be da shoes!"

The spots were more than a way to sell Air Jordans. They represented a cultural moment that forced us to look at sport and apparel through a different lens. Now, decades later, Spike Lee is still challenging our perspectives.

A little while ago, Spike showed up on the streets of New York with a different kind of message. It was in a CloudCoin commercial.

Dressed as a carnival barker or Dixieland jazz musician, Spike hit us with a powerful line that struck me as rather poignant: "Our currency is not current."

While I didn't love what the ad was selling, the message leading up to the product pitch was insightful and important:

> **Our currency is not current…**
> **We call it green, but it's only white.**
> **Where's the women? The Black folks?**
> **And the people of color?**
> **Native Americans got a nickel—a nickel!…**
> **Seven million Americans have no bank account…**
> **Old money's not going to pick us up.**
> **It pushes us down…**
> **But new money? New money is positive.**
> **Inclusive.**
> **Fluid.**
> **Strong.**
> **Culturally rich.**
> **Where status is anything but status quo…**
> **The digital rebellion is here.**
> **Old money's out. New money is in.**

Spike hit us with a powerful line that struck me as rather poignant: "Our currency is not current."

When I heard the line "We call it green, but it's only white," the gulp in my throat was heard throughout the land. It's a pretty blunt reminder of how much of our economic system has failed to evolve with the times.

I think you could inject the word "business" to see a more holistic problem.

Our business isn't current.
Where are the women? The Black folks?
And the people of color?
Old business isn't going to pick us up.
It pushes us down.
But new business? New business is positive.
Inclusive.
Fluid.
Strong.
Culturally rich.
Where status is anything but status quo.
The rebellion is here.
Old business is out. New business is in.

Whether it's digital currencies, internet-only retailers, entertainment streamers, or any other disruptive offerings, rebels can push the rest of us to rethink the entire system. They represent a new era and a new definition of what business can be.

And what it needs to be.

Until it's not.

CloudCoin filed for Chapter 11 in 2023 with liabilities estimated between $100 and $500 million.

Bitcoin has been marred by a series of scandals, security breaches, and Ponzi schemes. A lot of it because it's not a member of the "system" where checks and balances prevent the widespread fraud we've seen.

In some ways, the revolution just had facelift. Which is consistent with where we've been before—businesses don't overhaul their practices; they just polish their messaging.

And what better polish could there be than a shiny new purpose statement?

Senior leaders were fighting reputation wars on multiple fronts.

And it was starting to get worse.

Pressure's On

Systemic legacies, poor decisions, and growing greed all created a justifiable crankiness among the 99 percent. Wealth inequality didn't just exist over the past decade; it flourished.

As wealth continues to accumulate at the top and the gap between the haves and have-nots widens, the pressure on have-nots intensifies. That leads to the kind of pushback we're starting to see.

Workers are beginning to revolt—and it's not limited to white-collar folks resisting return-to-office mandates, either. After decades of decline, unions are back.

Workers are feeling the squeeze of contemporary capitalism with stagnant wages, job insecurity, and income gaps. No surprise there's a resurgence in union-organizing efforts from warehouses to coffee shops.

Amazon warehouse workers, Starbucks baristas, Trader Joe's workers, and John Deere employees have all taken steps to unionize, demanding better working conditions and fairer wages. Actors and writers went on strike, pushing back against practices they see as exploitative and threatening to their livelihoods. Heck, even the Dartmouth men's basketball team voted to unionize.

According to the National Labor Relations Board, union representation petitions filed in fiscal year 2022 increased by 53 percent compared to the previous year. As we creative people say when we reference data, that's a lot.

In the eyes of some, it's one more reason to debate the latest definition of capitalism. The pressure on businesses to do and be better isn't just coming from leaders; it's coming from the ground up.

Cha Gheill!

I have two undergraduate degrees from Queen's University, the finest academic institution in the land: a Bachelor of Arts and a Bachelor of Physical and Health Education. Like most business thinkers, and writers who own an ad agency, I was a phys-eddy.

Weirdly, I have never actually worked in phys ed. My first job was helping to launch the national executive MBA program in the business school at Queen's, before it was officially known as the Smith School of Business. From sports to business. I don't have an MBA, but after sitting through every class of an entire program, I certainly feel like I do. And if you don't believe me, I have a ton of khakis and golf shirts to prove it.

Recently, under the visionary tagline "This Is Business Now," Smith School of Business launched a campaign that resonated far beyond the university's limestone academic halls and into the very fabric of modern capitalism. Karen Howe, a wonderful and talented person I've always liked and admired, lead the creative thinking on it.

One ad read:

> **From next quarter to next generation.**
> **This is business now.**

Business isn't hoping to move from short-term wins to long-term impact.

It's already there. This is business *now*. Not "This is where business is going."

This campaign was a call to arms, urging business leaders and aspiring entrepreneurs to think beyond immediate financial returns and consider the broader implications of their actions.

Another ad read:

> **From net earnings to net zero. This is business now.**

They were challenging companies to redefine their success by their contributions to achieving net-zero emissions and fostering a sustainable future. Hey, if we don't have a planet, it doesn't really matter how great the camera is on your mobile device, does it?

The world had changed, and Smith was at the forefront, leading the conversation on how businesses could adapt and thrive in the new reality. This wasn't about corporate social responsibility as an afterthought but as a core business strategy.

As we navigate the complexities of all this chaos, the lessons from Smith School of Business are clear: Adapt, innovate, and embrace a broader definition of success.

This is the future of business, and it's happening now.
If only leaders were clear on how to realize it.

Keeping Score

If you're keeping score, right now business leaders are like cats chasing laser pointers.

They leap.
They lunge.
They twist.
They turn.

And they're left exhausted and empty-pawed when the game ends.

This is what they're being bombarded with:

A global pandemic that refuses to fully go into hiding, leaving behind a trail of uncertainty and disruption. An economic landscape that features inflation, supply chain snarls, and the looming threat of recession. Geopolitical tensions and conflicts that ripple through markets and disrupt trade. A workforce that's demanding more than pay. They want purpose, flexibility, and a voice. How dare they?

A societal reckoning with social injustice and inequality. The relentless march of technological advancement, with AI and automation transforming industries and amplifying stress. The climate crisis, demanding urgent action and sustainable practices.

A relentless 24/7 news cycle and social media echo chamber that amplifies every misstep and fuels outrage.

Leaders are white-knuckling it, trying to keep their organizations on track while the world seems determined to throw them off course. They're being blamed for everything, expected to solve something, and they can't focus on anything.

They're sitting at their desks. They're disheveled and exhausted.

There's a knock at the door. A buzz of a text message. And a notification of an email. They wearily lift up their heads in nervous anticipation of the latest headline, complaint, or expectation and say, "Now what?"

3

"If at first you don't succeed,

you need better lead gen."

NAPOLEON BONAPARTE

NOW WHAT? GROWTH'S WHAT

People want to do the right thing. They just don't know what the right thing is.

Get In the Driver's Seat

Picture this: a lone office chair, pristine white, strapped down with full-body seat belts against a pale green backdrop. That's the cover of the *Harvard Business Review* from September 2022.

The headline? "Strategies for Turbulent Times."

Now, if HBR had any sense of humor, maybe the headline would've read "Strap In, Kids. This Is Gonna Be a Shit Show." Alas, HBR isn't known for humor, let alone a potty mouth. So we'll stick with "Strategies for Turbulent Times."

Who signed up for this chaotic roller coaster, anyhow? Leaders did.

They're the ones in the driver's seats. And while it's undeniably tough, the overwhelming sentiment I get from leaders is one not of defeat but of frustration.

They want to be successful and sell a lot of stuff and make a lot of money for their people, board, and investors. They want to explore new technologies and AI. They want to drive sustainability. They want to respect human rights and achieve equality. They want to save the world, feed the hungry, and more.

But how do they do it? They certainly have plenty of options for information and inspiration. But it's easy to get lost in a maze of well-intentioned advice. Leaders are bombarded with books, LinkedIn posts, and TED Talks, all promising simple methodologies, breakthrough ideas, and proprietary processes that will magically transform chaos into delight. They read, they listen, they attend conferences, they hire consultants, they join think tanks and mastermind groups... all in a desperate search for the answer.

But at the end of the day, they're no closer to finding it. They're still lost, still frustrated, still unsure.

This is the defining paradox of leadership today, and the very reason I felt compelled to write this book:

People want to do the right thing. They just don't know what the right thing is.

As strategist Glen Markham hinted, it's like every business leader is channeling the Clash's Joe Strummer belting about whether he should stay or go.

> **People want to do the right thing.**
> **They just don't know what the right thing is.**

That's where purpose comes in. Not the kind of purpose that's plastered on a corporate website or splashed across a billboard. It's not the kind that checks boxes, saves kittens, or plants trees. It's the kind that's deeply ingrained in the DNA of an organization. The kind that guides every decision, every action, every interaction. The kind that's not about making a profit, but about making a difference *while* you make a profit.

It's time for leaders to stop chasing the latest fads and quick fixes. It's time to stop outsourcing their responsibility to consultants and gurus. It's time to get back in the driver's seats and start steering their organizations toward a future that's not just purposeful but profitable.

Because in the end, the right thing isn't always easy and it's not always clear. But it's always worth fighting for.

Going Gaga for Leadership

At the 94th Academy Awards, the glamour of Hollywood's biggest night was overshadowed by a touching moment of genuine humanity.

Lady Gaga was presenting the Oscar for Best Picture with the legendary 76-year-old Liza Minnelli. They didn't approach the podium like most others. The lights came up and they were just there—already onstage.

Liza was sitting in a wheelchair. Gaga was standing by her side.

Liza is a beloved icon, and everyone—including me—was hoping for the best. She had been out of the public spotlight for quite some time, and I think we all wanted to see that high-octane, jazz-hands, entertainment-royalty spirit that we had come to associate with her confident and energetic personality.

As they began to deliver the important setup to the announcement of the nominees, it became clear that Liza was having difficulty reading her printed notes, finding her words, and using the teleprompter.

No one wanted to witness a person so famous and so cherished stumble through. Seeing someone born to perform have difficulty saying a few sentences under the lights was not easy. But it wasn't a judgment on my part.

It was a reminder. A reminder that eventually we'll all face such difficulties.

With millions of people watching at the apex of the show, for the biggest award of the night, I remember thinking to myself, "Oh no."

I could feel the tension in the room, and I wasn't even *in* the room.

Then, as if scripted by the cosmos, Lady Gaga leaned over to Liza and whispered, "I got you." Liza responded, "I know."

Three small words. "I got you."

Spoken with warmth. Spoken with assurance.

They did more than simply guide Liza through the moment. They demonstrated what true leadership looks like.

In the middle of an event characterized by individual achievement and recognition, Lady Gaga's actions stood out as a spotlight on empathy. Instead of drawing attention to herself, she focused on the person next to her, ensuring Liza felt comfortable and valued. This wasn't about the award or the spectacle. It was about human connection. It was about kindness. And it was about creating a moment to improve the situation that was unfolding before her.

There are about one million different definitions of leadership, and this is mine:

> **Leadership is taking specific actions based on the information you have before you to improve the lives of the people around you.**

That's it.

Leadership is taking specific actions based on the information you have before you to improve the lives of the people around you.

Let's break it down:

It's specific actions.
Leadership is about doing stuff.
Leadership is about behavior.
Leadership is about actions.
Leadership is a verb.

But those actions have to be based on something, and far too many leaders base their actions on what they've done in the past. Their choices are based on a world that doesn't even exist anymore. Past successes should rarely dictate present solutions because so many variables have changed along the way.

That's why the second part of that definition is so important. Leadership isn't just actions. Leadership is taking *specific* actions that are based on the information before you.

That information may be sales data. It may be body language. It may be an economic forecast. It might be a report. It might be a SWOT analysis done by an overpaid consultant, who is repackaging the very things that your team told them. Whatever it is, that information should inspire and inform a response. Responses are usually decisions, actions, or behaviors.

But why do we do it? We do it to improve the lives of people around us.

Sure, that means our customers.

But it also means that we do it to improve the lives of our people.

We do it to improve the lives of our partners.

We do it to improve the lives of our family.

    Lady Gaga embodied this definition of leadership perfectly.

When it comes to our work lives,
we don't need more egos.
We don't need more leads.
We don't need more policies.
And we don't need more promises.
We need more leaders.
And leaders need more growth.

Growth Is Good

While I'm an alum of Queen's and am very proud of the work our team did to launch an innovative executive education program, there are other schools I've always respected. University of Toronto's biz school is one of them.

During Roger Martin's tenure as dean of the Rotman School of Management, he executed a growth strategy that transformed the institution into a leading global business school. But he didn't just improve their reputation, increase their research output, or increase enrollment.

He grew revenue.

Over his 15 years as dean, he grew Rotman's revenue by 10 times. (I'd say "10X" but I wouldn't want Roger's work to be confused with Grant Cardone's sales-bro-focused descriptor.) He fundamentally altered the school's trajectory, and his approach is a powerful example of why growth isn't just a nice-to-have. It's essential for any organization.

Roger's strategy was rather simple *and* brilliant: Instead of reallocating existing resources and creating internal conflict, he focused on generating new revenue streams and then used that revenue to fund strategic priorities.

I know firsthand the challenges of working in academia—especially when you haven't been blessed with a PhD in some obscure and narrow topic ridiculously removed from the subject at hand. You think working with partners at a law firm is tough? Try giving the partners tenure, three letters after their names, and a pent-up desire for you to address them as "Doctor."

We don't need more egos. We need more leaders. And leaders need more growth.

Law firms and accounting firms don't even come close to the hazards of working in academia. As a nonacademic, Roger knew this. His approach allowed him to bypass the traditional battles over budget allocations. All the existing departments and programs continued to receive their usual funding. New initiatives were fueled by new revenue.

In my mind, Roger simply did what he had to do to achieve growth.

Surrounded by chaos, distracted by problems, lulled into a sense of paralysis by too many options before them, leaders should do one thing and one thing only:

Focus on growth.

That's it.

Focus On Growth

As Roger put it, "Growth solves many problems. It is like grease for an engine—it makes everything go with less friction... Everything is just easier with growth!"

As we learned from this Rotman School of Management example, growth enables institutions and organizations to expand their influence, attract top talent, and introduce groundbreaking products, services, and initiatives, without the internal friction that can often accompany change.

Just look at the remarkable run of Amazon. Now, in some ways, Amazon is becoming the new Apple—appearing as a go-to case and example in blog posts, speeches, and business books from people like me. On one hand, Amazon may have become a business cliché. On the other, we'd be idiots if we didn't glance in their direction to see what worked for them.

In the early years, Amazon's focus on really rapid growth allowed it to scale quickly, diversify its product offerings, and enter new markets. Growth gave them a *Harry Potter* invisibility cloak of protection from any competition and gave them the resources needed for innovation and acquisition. In the middle of the huge growth spurt, they launched Amazon Web Services *and* acquired Whole Foods.

It seemed like each new growth spurt fueled the next. Along the way, Amazon was able to gradually improve operations and customer experience *and* simultaneously reinvest in and redefine itself. I think that's called "the sweet spot."

Don't forget about talent, either. As organizations expand, new roles emerge from the chaos. Someone has to sort out who does what. What an amazing opportunity for some people to step into leadership positions. I think a lot of my growth came when I was allowed to lead something simply because I put my hand up. When there's trust and a path to career development, why would people leave? A culture of upward mobility is fun, exciting, exhausting, and something many want to be a part of.

Google's explosive growth created a whole whack of new opportunities for its engineers and managers. Google's a client of our agency, and this is happening again with its drive into AI. It's a wonderful culture. People *want* to work there. And once there, they want to stay.

Growth isn't just a target. It's the heartbeat of any thriving business. And that's the thing about heartbeats—they should never stop. Great leaders know growth isn't a one-off. It's a relentless and ongoing pursuit. The path may be messy, but the approach is simple: Keep growing.

There's just one thing to keep in mind: Growth isn't only about boosting the bottom line. It's about rethinking all the inputs that contribute to it.

The New Definition of Growth: Beyond the Bottom Line

Picture it. A salesperson sits before you in a meeting. After the normal opening chitchat and an awkward silence that acts as a segue to the real reason you're where you are, the salesperson clasps their hands in front of them, stares into your eyes, and says, "Soooo, what keeps you up at night?"

It's a question that automatically induces an eye roll from me.

Usually, because it's said with an air of importance, as if they're the first one to ever think of asking it. But more than that, it's because I know that my answer will be twisted into a response that justifies whatever it is the person is selling.

"Oh, profit keeps you up at night? I hear that a lot. I bet if you had qualified leads from your LinkedIn content that you could get the shut-eye you deserve. Fortunately, that's in our wheelhouse at LeadsSoYouCanSleep.com."

Whenever someone asks me, "What keeps you up at night?" I want to say,

> **Me?** Too much caffeine consumption, a deep concern that my children won't have a planet to inhabit, and wondering why I had to use all six attempts for this morning's Wordle. But it's probably just from watching TikTok videos right before getting into bed. Anyhoooo, would you look at the time. I had a hard stop three minutes ago...

IMHO, the more appropriate question to ask is "What are your priorities for the upcoming year?" When asked that recently, CEOs said growth more than anything else.

In Gartner's research, 62 percent of CEOs selected growth as their top business priority in 2024—the highest it's ranked since 2014 and an increase from the previous year's survey, where 49 percent of CEOs said their top business priority was growth.

They didn't define it as old-school financial growth, either. To them, it was about navigating a world where disruption is lurking around every corner. Think AI, supply chain snarls, and that pain-in-the-ass thing called climate change.

CEOs want to grow, but they also want to make sure their companies aren't swept away by the next tidal wave of change.

Traditionally, growth has been all about the dollars and synonymous with financial metrics. Leaders aimed for increases in top-line revenue and enhanced profitability.

How's that working out? Well, not so well, it seems.

Many Western countries are grappling with a productivity crisis, a phenomenon that can be traced back to organizations neglecting the holistic growth of their systems, people, technology, processes, and more. It's like trying to build a skyscraper on a foundation of sand—eventually, it's bound to crumble.

When they should have been playing the long game of growth, they were playing the short game of profits and dividends.

It's all just a reflection of outdated mindsets and a lack of investment in the very things that drive sustainable growth. In an era of rapid technological advancement, companies that cling to archaic systems and inefficient processes are destined to fall behind. You can't win an F1 race with a horse and buggy.

The McKinsey Global Institute has painted a rather stark picture of the potential consequences of this productivity slump. The message is clear: We can't afford to ignore it. We need to invest in infrastructure, education, research and development, and technology. We need to empower our workforce, foster innovation, and

Growth isn't defined by the dollars piling up.

create a culture of continuous learning and improvement. Only then can we hope to achieve sustainable economic growth.

We need to grow to grow.
The narrow definition of growth
is increasingly outdated.

Welcome to the new era, where growth isn't only about financial gains but about advancing every aspect of your business. It's about optimizing your systems, processes, approaches, and people so that financial success follows naturally.

Systems growth creates financial growth.
People growth creates financial growth.
Efficiency growth creates financial growth.
Team dynamics growth creates financial growth.
Customer experience growth creates financial growth.
E-commerce growth creates financial growth.

Growth isn't defined by the dollars piling up. It's defined by the progression and advancement of all the key components of your business that make financial success inevitable.

Focus on growing in all the right ways, and the financial success will take care of itself. Just one thing: None of it happens unless you start with you.

Swapping Out a *W* for an *M*

As a host and speaker, I've been a part of more corporate off-sites than you can shake a $40 convention center muffin at. I love them (the off-sites, not the muffins). The energy, the excitement, a bunch of 42-year-olds away from the office and sequestered from their spouses and children. It's enough to make you downright giddy at the thought of a good night's sleep.

Still, nothing pulls a team together like actually *getting* together. Nothing builds a team like having the entire team in the same place. There's nothing that says "I trust and support you" like colleagues saying "No, *you're* the best!" after one too many bottles of the taco-buffet cabernet.

After this many years, I know the flow. Outside the room, banners introducing that year's theme flap wildly, aided by the convention center air-conditioning. People are ushered in with walk-in music that gets their feet tapping and their hearts racing. Like a high school assembly, the last rows get filled first, the cliques stake their territory, and the keeners sit in the front row. When everyone is in place, the lights go dim and a Voice of God introduces the most senior person in the room.

As a 1980s yacht rock hit plays as walk-up music, the leader makes their way to the onstage podium wearing a T-shirt with the conference's theme on it and exclaims how excited they are to be there. Most of them genuinely are, too.

After walking the team through the year in review, they'll chart the organization's course for the next year with strategic priorities. Then they'll ditch the slides, step away from the podium, and begin what I like to call the "We need" wail.

We need to be better.
We need to deliver.
We need to focus.
We need to come together.
We need to be creative.
We need to collaborate.
We need to be one team.
We need to innovate.

We. We. We. We. We.

Sure, it's critical. I don't blame them and do the same myself. But the second half of the message is always missed. If the "we" doesn't become a "me," none of those statements will ever come true and the organization will never be in a position to reach its goals.

Earlier, I said that leadership was about improving the lives of our people and our partners and even our family members. But it's also about your life.

If you can't take actions based on the information before you to improve your own life, I don't have the confidence you can do it for other people.

All that growth that I spoke of—the systems growth, process growth, people growth, etc.—only occurs when it is preceded by personal growth. When individuals put their hands up and commit to growing as human beings and as leaders—trying new things, doing new things, creating new things. When individuals put their egos side and step outside their comfort zones to change what they do on a daily basis, then all the other growth can occur.

Because when people grow, teams grow.
When teams grow, departments grow.
When departments grow, organizations grow.
When organizations grow, communities grow.
When communities grow, its businesses can grow.

But it all starts with the person. It begins with "me" before becoming "we." We all want more from our businesses. But shouldn't we want more from ourselves, too?

Growth Is Blowin' in the Wind

It's tough enough convincing yourself to grow a little, let alone trying to convince other people that they should buy in to or support your growth. When you evolve, it can be a subtle reminder that they're not growing.

Let's face it. A lot of people are comfortable with the status quo. They're content with simply knowing what to expect from a situation or from a person. "When my boss does this, I do this and I get this result." When a leader indicates that they're going to invest in doing things differently for themselves, the team around them knows that before long, they will be personally impacted. Simply put, when leaders grow, there are direct effects on everyone around them.

Why do you think your team hates when you go to a conference or company-wide meeting?

Oh, they may act happy as you walk out the door with your carry-on suitcase rolling behind you. They may wish you well, tell you to enjoy yourself and to get some sun. But as soon as you pull away in an Uber, the people you leave behind immediately start complaining about what's going to happen when you return.

They've seen it before. And they expect it again. You're going to see three keynote speakers who will plant 20 wild ideas in your head. You're going to meet the C-suite, who will establish new expectations for your team. You're going to hear stories and case studies on how other regions and other divisions are outperforming yours. You're going to hear from your internal archnemesis on how amazing things are for them. And you're going to get new insight into decision-making from watching the blackjack table in the middle of Circus Circus.

Whatever it is, your team is counting down to the day you burst through the door and enthusiastically explain the million ideas you have that you want to get started on right away.

Bob Dylan's early success wasn't defined by audiences being unable to understand what he said—it would take years for him to develop that skill. His early grassroots success came from his socially conscious lyrics and simple acoustic guitar. Pepsi may have been the taste of a generation, but Dylan was the voice of a generation. People felt that he was channeling their inner angst, singing about the very things they believed in. He may have started as a darling of the folk music scene, but he eventually became a cultural icon.

Despite his success, Dylan felt constrained by the image that had created it. The landscape of America (and the world) was changing politically and socially. The idealism of the early 1960s was giving way to a more complex era, and Dylan believed that music—his music—needed to reflect that. Sticking to his acoustic roots felt to him like those people who refuse to give up their analog Rolodex; folk was waning, rock and roll was becoming the dominant genre, and electric guitars were the sound of the future.

Dylan knew that if he wanted to stay relevant to the world and true to his own artistic spirit, he needed to evolve. He needed to invest in personal growth (although I doubt he would have put it that way).

He once said, "An artist has got to be constantly in a state of becoming."

The same can be said for leaders.

His watershed moment came on July 25, 1965, at the Newport Folk Festival. Dylan took the stage with an electric guitar, backed by a full band. As the opening chords of "Maggie's Farm" rang out, boos and jeers erupted from the audience. The reaction wasn't one of love and support for the voice of a generation. It was one of shock and outrage at someone who didn't seem to get them. His "team" felt betrayed and accused Dylan of abandoning his roots and selling out.

And you thought convincing everyone to get on Slack was tough.

His audience had found comfort in and identified with his acoustic music. It represented a simpler vision of the world. And they didn't just want to live in that world. They wanted to be the ones to define it. They may not have "rocked" in that world, but they rocked that world. They thrived with Dylan leading them.

Despite the initial backlash, Dylan's decision to go electric proved to be a brilliant move. Sure, his electric albums like *Highway 61 Revisited*, *Bringing It All Back Home*, and *Blonde on Blonde* are critically celebrated and were financially successful. But more than that, I think Dylan going electric is the reason we're still talking about him now. His desire for growth and his insight into why he needed to evolve ensured his relevance and longevity in music. Had he remained strictly an acoustic artist, I don't think we'd be talking about him.

> **Leadership is taking specific actions based on the information you have before you to improve the lives of the people around you.**

I doubt Dylan looked at sales data, McKinsey reports, or 360-degree feedback when he invested in growth. He felt the change around him, decided to take personal action for growth, and led his people toward a better future even though they didn't want him to.

Dylan's electric transformation solidified his legacy. And your growth can solidify yours.

We are all works in progress.

I Should Be More, Shouldn't I?

The most repeated and referenced lines in business over the past hundred years or so should live in some hall of fame. Up front, you'd see Warren Buffett's "It takes 20 years to build a reputation and five minutes to ruin it." Beside it would be Peter Drucker's "The best way to predict the future is to create it" and William Gibson's "The future is already here—it's just not very evenly distributed."

But right up there with them would be a line from the wonderful Marshall Goldsmith: "What got you here won't get you there."

It's not only the title of his phenomenally successful book from 2007 (officially *What Got You Here Won't Get You There: How Successful People Become Even More Successful!* by Marshall Goldsmith with Mark Reiter). It's a line that's been repeated by speakers and executives since the book came out.

It's brilliant. It's insightful. It's simple. It's repeatable. It's just a great line. And the thinking behind the line? It's even better. The very skills, habits, and strategies that propelled you to your current level of achievement may not be the skills, habits, and strategies to propel you further.

In a great article in *Chief Executive* written with Kelly Goldsmith, Marshall shared a story from his own life involving one of his mentors, Dr. Paul Hersey. After heaping compliments and positive words about his professional relationships, Dr. Hersey said something that stopped Marshall in his tracks:

> **You are completely screwing up. You are running around like a chicken with your head cut off! You are selling the same thing day after day after day. You are not thinking, you are not writing and you are not developing new material. If you continue doing what you are now, you will have a successful life, but you will never become the person you could be—and you will regret it. You can be more.**

You can be more. You can be more.

We all want more from our businesses. More growth, more innovation, more impact. But shouldn't we want more from ourselves, too? As leaders, we often focus on pushing our companies, but we don't really push ourselves.

We are all works in progress. No matter how successful you may be, there is always room for improvement. We need to shed the illusion of perfection and embrace the messy, imperfect reality of growth.

I've had a series of Bo Burnham moments in my life when I totally reinvented myself, achieving personal growth (and some success) as a result. From a poor kid living in the south end of Oshawa to a PE grad to working at a business school to joining a web shop at the start of the internet to working in advertising to performing stand-up comedy to writing a play to becoming a creative director to becoming a speaker to writing a couple of books to starting my own agency to... blah blah, you get the point. I have resisted any hint of resignation and have avoided doing the same old thing.

Well... until I desperately needed it most.

The World Health Organization declared the global pandemic on March 11, 2020. On March 12, 2020, the day after the declaration of the pandemic, all I did was receive emails from Speakers Spotlight about all the guaranteed speaking revenue I had booked for the year that said "Cancel. Cancel. Reschedule. On hold. Cancel. Cancel."

I did 73 speaking engagements in 2019, and 2020 was booking in similar fashion, so you can probably do some rough math on the amount of money that walked out the door that day.

I lost all the speaking engagements. I wasn't sure what our clients were going to do or if I still had an agency. I wasn't sure how we were going to protect our people as we entered the turbulent time. Oh, and our house was under a massive renovation.

After having fought and clawed my way to a place of financial comfort, I thought I was about to lose it all. I thought that someone from the ruling class was going to show up, tap me on my shoulder, and send me back to the urine-filled stairwells of the apartment building on Wentworth Street in the south end of Oshawa.

At 3 a.m. that night, my wife came down.

> CHRISTY: What are you still doing up??
> ME: I'm doing the math.
> CHRISTY: Well, we have to go to a hospital immediately.

We did. And a few hours later, at 9:45 a.m. on March 13, 2020, we welcomed our second son, Benny, into the world. What joy! What happiness! Umm... What stress!

At 11 a.m. from the cafeteria of St. Michael's Hospital, I didn't call my family to announce the arrival of our child. I called my wealth advisor and my private banker. On one hand, I was experiencing one of the greatest joys of my life. On the other, I was filled with worry, shame, and a fear that for the first time, things wouldn't work out for the best. They'd work out for the worst.

It wasn't that what got me here wouldn't get me there.

It was that what got me here *couldn't* get me there.

At that point, before any hint of virtual delivery had even been contemplated, a lot of what I had done was no longer an option.

I should be more? Gulp.

I just assumed I was going to be less.

Mentally, I wasn't in a good place. And that led to a great resignation.

On the outside, I was pasting on a smile for my family and an optimistic tone for my colleagues. But on the inside, I was resigned to let whatever was going to happen happen, which is rarely listed in one of those "These are the top five things billionaires do before breakfast" articles.

I was in an emotional slump, and even though the world had drastically changed before me, I didn't proactively do anything to win the moment. There was a bunch of stuff that I had to stop doing—speaking, traveling, meeting—but I didn't want to explore what I had to *start* doing in response.

After some inspiration that I'll get into later, I invested in personal growth.

I knew that I needed a way to inspire and inform people from the comfort of my own house. So, I did.

I began crafting the content I would cover if given the chance. What *should* I tell people? What did my team need to hear? What did they want to hear? What about clients? What advice would I (and we) give them? And how the hell would I deliver it?

I pulled an all-nighter. I dove deep into learning new software, I set up a studio environment in my house, and I bought new equipment. I learned an entirely new approach, and given that some of my content was about hotels and airlines, I scoured the world for inspiring stories to share. Before long, I worked on the first virtual program for a big bank, I volunteered to speak at one of the first Speakers Spotlight virtual sessions, and we pitched to help the wonderful team at MediaSmarts create a national campaign to stop misinformation about COVID.

The growth was uncomfortable *and* liberating. It was exhausting *and* rejuvenating. It was painful *and* the exact remedy I needed. I needed to be more. I had to be more. For me, for our clients, for our team, and—most importantly—for my family.

We can all be more. I only hope that we don't have to go through that again to realize it.

4

"To err is human.

To blame it on spotty Wi-Fi is divine."

ARISTOTLE

**THINK
DO
SAY
GROW**

Leadership is taking specific actions based on the information you have before you to improve the lives of the people around you.

Driving Growth

I've mentioned that I grew up in Oshawa, Ontario. I don't know if it still does, but at one point the city sign read "Oshawa. The City That Moto-Vates Canada." That's how big an impact and influence General Motors had on the town. The Junior A hockey team that greats such as Bobby Orr and Eric Lindros played for was called the Oshawa Generals. That's almost as bad as Anaheim's nod to Disney with the Mighty Ducks.

That was then, this is now. Oshawa has diversified, and GM isn't what GM used to be.

A couple of years ago, GM found itself grappling with an array of challenges: The rise of Tesla and other EVs. The proliferation of ride-share programs. The sophistication of new car rental offerings. A fragile economy. A growing perception that combustion engine cars are the villains in the climate crisis. Add in the lingering stench of its 2008–09 bailout request delivered by executives who flew on a private jet to beg the government for more money, and you can see that one thing was clear:

GM needed to be more.

If they wanted to grow financially, they had to grow holistically.

They needed to rethink who they were, what they did, and how they presented themselves to the market.

So how did they do it?

They Were Focused by Purpose

Lazy executives might jump straight to "Let's make the logo more contemporary," but better executives, ahem, know better.

True transformation begins with the purpose behind why you're doing it in the first place. Before 2021, GM's mission statements had grown stale and disconnected from the rapidly evolving ecosystem around them. Besides, they had missions and visions and purpose statements and more. The first critical step was to redefine purpose in a way that resonated both internally and externally.

They knew that they needed a collective commitment and approach to shaping the future of mobility, the future of the company, the future of work, and the future of the planet.

They got there with the statement "We stand together to drive the world forward."

As a purpose, it does everything it needs to. It reinforces the need to be united and for collaboration. It prioritizes progress and innovation. And it establishes a shared purpose that can connect GM to communities inside and outside the organization. While the inclusion of "drive" is a nice nod to their core product, it also symbolizes momentum and advancement. Purpose should be the strategic heartbeat of an organization, and this purpose statement certainly did that.

The purpose part? Check.

They Were Defined by Their Actions

GM understood that a well-intentioned line was useless without real action. But I'm sure they probably also knew that that a bunch of random activities—Go electric! Use AI! Create a TikTok account! Optimize the supply chain!—were a recipe for disaster, chaos, and confusion.

To truly drive growth, GM had to fundamentally change the way they operated, using their purpose statement, "We stand together to drive the world forward," as a guide for how to do it. So, they did.

They drove the dealership customer experience forward. They seamlessly blended digital options with in-person interactions for a frictionless and enjoyable experience. They implemented digital showrooms, created virtual test-drives, and allowed customers to explore vehicles in new and innovative ways.

They drove social impact forward. To create a winning and contemporary culture, GM committed to building a diverse, equitable, and inclusive team. I know you've read that line before, and you'd be justified if it just induced an eye roll, but this didn't seem like a box-checking exercise. They launched initiatives to increase representation, and they partnered with organizations like the National Society of Black Engineers to ensure they had a pipeline of diverse talent.

They drove workplace innovation forward. GM didn't just ask for unity. They championed better ways of working and improved internal collaboration with employees and their vast network of partners, vendors, and suppliers. They also held regular town halls to keep communication transparent and inclusive. Not rocket science (or car science), but certainly something that organizations (including my own) don't do enough of.

They drove their products forward. GM revolutionized their product lineup with advanced platforms and cutting-edge technology that included electric and autonomous vehicles. This (not so) simple move had a win-win effect. It enhanced customer pride of ownership *and* it helped GM contribute to a healthier planet.

They drove advanced platforms forward. GM's vision is a world with zero crashes, zero emissions, and zero congestion. And during this process, they took significant strides toward achieving that vision. They expanded the definition of "sustainability" beyond the usual green-focused meaning to include sustainable people and the creation of livable and sustainable cities. They invested in smart city initiatives and vehicle-to-everything technology to enhance urban mobility and safety.

They drove enterprise efficiency forward. Obviously, GM is a huge company with a massive footprint and an ability to scale that's more significant than most others in the entire world. Knowing this, GM leveraged their manufacturing capabilities, global scale, and collaborations to modernize their inventory model and logistics. They adopted Industry 4.0 technologies, such as IoT and AI, to streamline production and reduce waste, and that resulted in cost savings and environmental benefits.

They thought about it. They did it. The only thing left to do was to sell it.

And by "sell it," I mean communicate what they believed and what they did in a way that made others want to join them in the journey.

True growth occurs when others adopt your ideas and passions.

It Was Adopted through Communication

True growth occurs when others—both inside and outside the organization—adopt your ideas and passions. Adoption usually depends on how you communicate what you believe and what you do. And first impressions are critical to winning them over.

Remember that old GM logo? The big capital *G* and *M* in a box of blue that was so dated you could smell the carburetor on it? Yeah. That had to change. It no longer represented their purpose, so they embarked on and started their organizational transformation with a visual transformation.

The blue was lightened to appear more modern, the *G* and *M* were changed to lowercase letters to reduce the perceived arrogance, and an electric plug was subtly embedded in the negative space of the *M*. Nothing says "We're electric" like a plug in your logo.

Yes, these changes were cosmetic.
But they were also a declaration of their new identity.

Their purpose, "We stand together to drive the world forward," helped focus their activities and decisions, but it wasn't a great line to lead with as a summary of everything they were doing. From a strategic perspective, it's a great line, but I don't think it's simple or inspiring or punchy enough to bring others on board. So they changed that, too.

"We stand together to drive the world forward" became "Everybody in."

Everybody in.

Now that's a line that can inspire. It's simple and inclusive and it probably resonates with both internal and external audiences. It invited everyone to be part of the journey. Personally, I would have preferred if they had opted to use the line "Get in, loser, we're going shopping" (*Mean Girls!*) but alas, "Everybody in" it is.

Their new approach to communication wasn't just about telling people what they were doing. It was about showing them. GM launched a series of high-profile campaigns that showcased their new EV lineup, promoted their environmental initiatives, and shone a light on their commitment to diversity and inclusion. And all the stuff they did outside was matched by impressive work inside.

GM recognized that true transformation is an inside job. They held workshops and training sessions to help educate employees about the new purpose and how it impacted everyone's day-to-day work. The purpose drove growth in the sense of ownership, pride, and company culture.

GM drove purpose forward.
They drove experience forward.
They drove culture forward.
They drove innovation forward.
But more than anything, they drove growth forward.
They made growth the heart of their business.
And they did it by being focused by purpose,
defined by their actions, and adopted through
compelling communications.

Put another way, their growth was driven by what they thought, what they did, and what they said.

Thinking Doing Saying

My last book, *Think Do Say*, offered a powerful framework for seizing attention and building trust in a crowded marketplace—so much so that I put "How to Seize Attention and Build Trust in a Busy, Busy World" right in the subtitle. If you don't believe me, I encourage you to buy a copy. Right now. Liquidation sale.

I always thought Think Do Say—the concept, not the book—was more than that. Since the book was written, we have used TDS at my agency, Church+State, as a total operating system for us and our clients, including Google, DoorDash, UNICEF, Walmart, and many others. We've used TDS to frame and drive transformation consulting, brand redesigns, internal communications strategies, training and development, and traditional advertising campaigns. I'd throw "and make lasagna" in there, but my family would disown me.

Leaders need to counter chaos with simplicity. When it comes to growth, TDS is how you do it. The goals are different, the inputs are different, and the results are different. But the process should be similar.

Think: Focused by Purpose

Purpose is the compass guiding growth, not the flag waving for attention.

It's an organization's strategic heartbeat, and it should inform every action and decision within an organization. When a company is bound by purpose, it transcends profits and creates real value for customers, employees, and community.

In marketing (and in my last book), a well-defined purpose helps brands capture attention and build trust because others know you believe in something that goes beyond your products. To most people, that's refreshing.

But the role of purpose in growth is quite different. It's not about capturing attention; it's about capturing focus. It's not about winning the battle for time with purpose-based messaging. It's about winning the battle for growth with the best purpose-focused actions and priorities to do it. GM didn't grow because a talented writer or strategist created "We stand together to drive the world forward." GM grew because of the initiatives that "We stand together to drive the world forward" helped create.

Purpose isn't a slogan. It's the fuel for growth.

Do: Defined by Actions

Purpose without specific actions is meaningless. The actions that a company takes are what brings their purpose to life and what creates exceptional experiences for everyone involved. There are a million ways to grow yourself and your business. The lens I see growth through can be loosely defined as "experience"—for you, for your team, for your partners, for your prospects, and for your customers and clients. Frictionless experiences that reinforce a fundamental belief lead to growth.

This is where the "Do" part of Think Do Say comes into play. Actions speak louder than words, and they are the true measure of a company's commitment to its purpose.

I also think it's a pretty good indicator of how good the growth will be, too.

GM demonstrated their purpose through tangible changes and very specific initiatives. And all of them reinforced the very idea of driving progress.

They thought it. They did it.
But they still needed to convince people to join them.

Say: Adopted through Communications

It's not enough to simply think and do. You have to say it in a way that resonates with your audience enough that they want to join you in your journey. There are enough crappy communications filled with pitch-slapping tactics, out-of-touch narratives, and empty promises out there. Effective communication is the bridge that connects purpose and actions with a broader audience. Still...

You writing it doesn't mean they'll read it.
You sending it doesn't mean they'll open it.
You recording it doesn't mean they'll watch it.
You posting it doesn't mean they'll consume it.
You repeating it doesn't mean they'll embrace it.
You don't need to tell it so that they *have* to join you.
You need to sell it so that people *want* to join you.

Sell it, don't tell it.

GM's "Everybody In" campaign is a great case of how to adopt purpose and actions through communication. Their job certainly wasn't complete with the writing of the line, and there were a ton of other effective communications that accompanied it. But on its own, it's a simple example of what needs to be done.

By crystallizing their purpose into an inclusive and memorable line, GM was able to effectively communicate their purpose to both internal and external audiences.

By focusing on these three pillars, companies can achieve sustainable growth that goes beyond financial metrics. They can build wonderful experiences and cultures and be as progressive as they should be, making TDS the ultimate guide for any organization looking to thrive in the modern world.

As leaders, you may ask yourself,
"What was I made for?"
This. You were made for this.

What Barbie Was Made For

In December 2023, I came down with (caught? got?) COVID for the second time. By then, I was a pro and knew exactly what to do. I retreated to and secluded myself in our third-floor guest bedroom so that I wouldn't directly interact with my wife or our children. I was down for the count for 36 hours or so, confined to my bed.

It was then, when I was fuzzy of mind, that I decided to watch the Barbie movie.

Look, if you know me, you know that I'm not some macho, testosterone guy's guy. I'm not handy. I'm not aggressive. And I don't change my own oil. It wasn't out of some dude code that I had avoided watching *Barbie*. I love the brand. I love the business. And I know what a positive role model Barbie has been not just for young girls but for young boys, too.

I don't know. I just thought the movie would be horrible.

It wasn't. It was fantastic.

As I lay there in my COVID stupor, Billie Eilish's inspiring voice kept singing in my head. All I could think about was my mom. And how I wish she were alive to hear the things that were being said (and sung).

THE PURPOSE OF PURPOSE

As a woman with spina bifida, who attended a school literally called the Montreal School for Crippled Children, who graduated in tenth grade, who was divorced from an alcoholic ex-husband and father to her four kids, who stayed home to raise her kids on government assistance (for a few years), and who later in life was admitted to hospital for depression as she started to question whether she had made the right life decisions for her children, I imagined that the song in her head would have been "What Was I Made For?"

I'm sure she also wondered, like Barbie, whether she had neglected her own happiness in favor of others, and if she could find it now.

If this brand could make me cry thinking of my mom, I can only imagine what it did for women. Wow.

Look, Barbie has been a cultural icon for over six decades. But as times changed, so did perceptions of the brand.

Barbie was often criticized for promoting unrealistic beauty standards and limiting gender roles. While everyone may want a beach house, I'm not sure everyone wanted to (or should want to) look like Barbie.

Barbie needed to grow if the business wanted to grow. It needed a fundamental makeover driven by purpose, defined by actions, and adopted through effective communication.

The Need for Change

The challenges facing Barbie were multifaceted. On one hand, there was increasing societal awareness about diversity, inclusion, and the harmful impacts of unrealistic body images. On the other, the toy market was becoming more competitive with the rise of digital entertainment and innovative toy brands. Besides, Barbie's legacy as a symbol of a bygone era was at odds with the progressive values of new generations.

Barbie faced a triple threat: evolving social values, a competitive toy market, and an outdated image. If they wanted to see growth, Mattel needed a makeover for more than just the doll.

Think: Focused by Purpose

Redefining Barbie's purpose was crucial to the growth. The purpose couldn't be about being a beloved toy or cultural icon, either. Whenever businesses look to their histories to justify their "presence" (see what I did there?), I think it's a cop-out. "But we're Barbie and people have loved us for years!" is a recipe for eventual and total irrelevance.

The purpose needed to be more specific, inclusive, and aspirational, while still being strategically tied to how Mattel made their money. And that's what they did.

Barbie's new purpose became about empowerment and representation:

> To inspire the limitless potential in every girl.

Barbie's purpose doesn't just drive organizational growth. It inspires personal growth to do it.

Now that's something that a parent like me could get behind. That's something that older women who wish they had that presence in their life could get behind. That's something I think my mom would have got behind.

It wasn't a tagline. It was a commitment.

It was a commitment to break down stereotypes and show that Barbie could be anything. It wasn't only relevant to existing fans, either. It appealed to a broader, more diverse audience. Funny how when you relate to more people, your potential market grows. It was everything it needed to be, and it reflected values of inclusivity and empowerment.

Do: Defined by Actions

Purpose without action is meaningless. For Barbie, this meant making tangible changes that embodied their new purpose.

One of the most obvious (and newsworthy) changes was the introduction of Barbies with different body types, skin tones, and abilities. Barbie launched dolls with curvier bodies, taller and shorter statures, and more realistic proportions. You know, like my body. They even introduced Barbies with vitiligo, a doll with a prosthetic limb, and a Barbie with Down syndrome.

From there, they extended their thinking to Barbies who represented real people. Real-life role models who had made significant contributions to society and who served as inspiration for young girls: Rosa Parks, Maya Angelou, and Billie Jean King were all created in Barbie form. Let's face it, if you want to inspire the limitless potential in every girl, celebrating those women who went beyond society's limitations is a great place to start. Barbie has since created 60 role model Barbies.

Through research, Mattel realized that much progress has been made when it comes to gender equality. The problem is that stereotypes and biases still exist, which get in the way of girls' trajectories. To combat that, they created the Dream Gap Project. It's dedicated to closing the gap by challenging gender stereotypes and helping to undo the biases that bar girls from becoming who they want to be. The initiative works with nonprofits and has developed school curriculum, too. Since it started, the Barbie Dream Gap Project has given over $2 million to nonprofit organizations that support girls and enable them to reach their full potential.

New products appeal to new people. That's purpose in action.

Barbie needed to grow if the business wanted to grow.

Say: Adopted through Communications

Sure, Barbie invested in a ton of great content through their YouTube channel. At the time of writing, they have 12.4 million subscribers.

But bigger than that, of course, is the movie.

Inspired by the brand's official tagline, "You can be anything," *Barbie* was directed by Greta Gerwig and starred Margot Robbie, Ryan Gosling, America Ferrera, Kate McKinnon, and others. It was more than entertainment. It was a cultural event designed to reframe Barbie's image. Hiring Gerwig as director was enough to better align Barbie with more contemporary values all on its own.

Look, of course Barbie sold instead of told in traditional and expected ways. They had amazing partnerships with influencers and other brands that complemented their purpose. They collaborated with Lizzo. Linked up with Airbnb, Forever 21, Gap, Crocs, L'Oréal, Pinkberry, Cold Stone Creamery, Ruggable, Bumble, and Bloomingdale's. They shared on Insta, created for TikTok, and engaged directly with their audience to build community.

But a movie? That people paid to see? That was brilliant and successful and helped me through a night of feverish sweats?

A movie was a killer move. But it was really the cherry on top of a Barbie sundae. The transformation of the business—through the lens of purpose—was growing long before the movie premiered.

Mattel reported double-digit growth in their Barbie segment. In 2021 alone, Barbie sales surged by 16 percent, its highest sales growth in over two decades. The success of the Barbie movie further cemented the brand's resurgence. It grossed over $1.4 billion worldwide, was a cultural phenomenon that transcended generations, and still makes me tear up when I think of it. And the Ken dance at the Oscars? *Gold.*

Sure, they sold more dolls and shipped more merch. But more than that, Barbie reaffirmed its status as a beloved and influential cultural icon in a far more relevant way.

Barbie's growth means girls can grow. And in fulfilling its purpose, "To inspire the limitless potential in every girl," Barbie is a textbook example of how a business fully understood the role that purpose can play and should play.

THE RUNNER
SAVANNAH BANANAS

In comedy, a sketch that appears sporadically throughout a show is called a "runner." Well, the Savannah Bananas is the perfect case study to be a runner in this book.

As you will see, I'm a bit of a baseball nut. So much so that I've been to spring training. Multiple times. On my own. I'll admit, I'm a bit of a traditionalist, and the Savannah Bananas are far from a typical baseball team. But even I have to say, they're worth cheering for.

Just go to a game and you'll see why.

They're a sports entertainment phenomenon that has flipped the traditional baseball model on its head, redefining what it means to play (and watch) the game.

Founded in 2016 by Jesse Cole, a former collegiate baseball player turned entrepreneur, the Savannah Bananas started as an ordinary collegiate summer league team that competed in the Coastal Plains League (CPL). But Jesse—with his audacious vision and signature yellow tuxedo—turned the team into an extraordinary example of disruptive sports marketing and incredible *The Purpose of Purpose*-worthy customer experience.

Jesse purchased the team—then faced with financial struggles and dwindling attendance—with a very clear mission: Save it from extinction. Ummmmm . . . He kind of overshot that goal a bit. Because what followed was a radical transformation: The Bananas became synonymous with fun, fan engagement, and a purpose-driven approach. They're a perfect example of how to achieve growth in a stagnant industry.

Throughout the book, we'll explore how the Savannah Bananas navigated a challenging landscape to not only become a viral sensation but to hit grand-slam growth in the process.

IN SEARCH OF GROWTH: WHY THEY NEEDED A PURPOSE AT ALL

For any teams not named Yankees or Dodgers, the words "baseball" and "growth" don't slide together so easily these days.

Baseball, once America's pastime, has been losing its grip on younger audiences. Competing for audience eyeballs with everything from video games and social media platforms to faster-paced sports, niche content, and Netflix, baseball is often viewed as yesterday's sport. New is exciting! And there's nothing new about baseball. In fact, most of baseball is resistant to bringing in anything new.

It's slow. It's old. It's traditional. And in a world that celebrates big brands and cherishes celebrities, the Coastal Plains League offers none of it. Unlike major league teams with massive marketing budgets and established fan bases or minor league teams attached to those teams with the "potential stars of tomorrow" appearing every night, the CPL operated on a more intimate scale. It was good baseball. But it wasn't exactly a direct path to playing for the Atlanta Braves. And with rosters changing every year, there was no player familiarity, no stars, and little emotional connection for fans to the product on the field.

Enter Jesse.

Jesse knew that if the team was going to survive—let alone thrive—they needed a fresh plan with better insights and stronger focus. Following the same rules wasn't going to cut it. He understood that to compete with the digital world and reengage fans in Savannah, the team, the operations, and the approach needed a complete overhaul.

The traditional model, with its focus on the game itself, was no longer enough. It wasn't about wins and losses.

The game was the game. Jesse saw a disconnect between the traditional baseball experience and the entertainment-hungry audiences of today. He knew—as do I—that audiences want more. They want a total fan experience.

And that's exactly what Jesse set out to provide.

But what kind of experience? How would he analyze and prioritize? His budget wasn't endless, his timing wasn't eternal, and his patience wasn't limitless.

He needed growth. And he would use a new and unique purpose to build it. At the end of the next chapter, we'll see what that purpose is.

5

"Work-life balance is a myth we tell ourselves between Zoom meetings."

BUDDHA

FOCUSED BY PURPOSE
(THE THINK PART)

Purpose isn't just the reason we exist—it's the framework for every decision we make.

A New Era Dawns—on Purpose

Back in 1970—the year I was born—Milton Friedman, a renowned University of Chicago economist and future Nobel Prize winner, wrote an article that is rather well known in the capitalist class.

"The Social Responsibility of Business Is to Increase Its Profits" was first published in the *New York Times Magazine* in September of that year. The piece argued that the only thing CEOs should focus on was making money for their shareholders.

Friedman argued that company executives weren't really executives at all. Hell, they were more like employees of the shareholders, and their responsibilities included whatever was best for them.

Purpose? Sure. They had a purpose. It's just that every business shared the same purpose: Put as much money into the pockets of their owners as possible.

Social problems? Not your job.

The environment? Leave it to the hippies.

Inclusivity? That didn't include you.

All the "better for the community" stuff was another way of saying "take money from shareholders without their permission."

Given most executives were also shareholders, this was not a difficult sell.

The result? The creation of shareholder primacy: Business leaders prioritize short-term dividends and shareholder returns over long-term growth and things like employee well-being, customer satisfaction, and the environment.

It wasn't up to the corporations to save the planet. The corporation's purpose was to drive profit for the company and returns for the shareholders. If the shareholders wanted to donate their money to environmental causes, they could. But a corporation doing so on their behalf was ill advised.

For close to 50 years, the private sector embraced Friedman's paper and prioritized shareholder value.

All until Fink made a stink.

Surrounded by all the issues we've already explored, Larry Fink, the CEO of the world's largest asset manager,

BlackRock, sent a powerful message to CEOs in his annual letter. This is what he wrote:

> Purpose is not the sole pursuit of profits but the animating force for achieving them. Profits are in no way inconsistent with purpose—in fact, profits and purpose are inextricably linked. As we enter 2019, commitment to a purpose will be a paramount factor in how we evaluate your companies... You risk losing our support if you don't focus on long-term strategies for value creation that are also aligned with positive societal impact.

Put more succinctly, align your business with a greater purpose, or we won't support you.

Gulp.

Fink's emphasis on the growing importance of ESG factors in investment decisions signaled a rather significant shift in investor priorities.

As if that wasn't a loud enough shot across the bow, the Business Roundtable, a group of 180 CEOs representing 35 percent of the total market cap in the US and chaired by the CEO of Walmart, got together in August 2019. In a letter to Senator Elizabeth Warren, they took Fink's sentiment even further and completely contradicted Friedman by declaring a new "Statement on the Purpose of a Corporation":

> Companies should serve not only their shareholders, but also deliver value to their customers, invest in employees, deal fairly with suppliers and support the communities in which they operate.

Put another way, shareholders were important, but they weren't the only constituent. Employees, customers, partners, and communities were all also important.

Not to be dramatic, but this was huge.

It signaled a departure from a narrow focus on shareholder value, which had dominated corporate decision-making for close to five decades. In its place was a definition of purpose that recognized the interconnectedness of business and society.

The greater good, it seemed, would be good for business.

Bad for Business, Good for Purpose

Oh, you were acknowledged as Employee of the Month at your local McDonald's in 1986 and got a glamour shot that your mother kept in her house until you were married? Be proud.

Jack Welch one-upped you. He was awarded Manager of the Century. Not at his local fast-food resto. For all businesses. In the entire world. I'm not sure if he got a headshot with the award or not.

One of the highlights of my career was getting to interview Jack Welch onstage at the Art of Management conference in 2012.

I'll be honest, I wanted to hate him.

Given his legacy and reputation as "Neutron Jack," his role as chief cheerleader for shareholder primacy, and the guy who famously fired the bottom 10 percent every year, I wanted to feel everything I thought a man of his stature deserved.

And then I met him.

He was charming, funny, honest, and explained his approach in a way that left me respecting (and liking) him more than I ever thought I would. I learned more in one hour of conversation than I did in entire semesters of school.

Sadly, Jack passed away in 2020, so he's not here to defend himself, which isn't exactly fair.

I think Jack was simply a product of his time. Had he had the insight about shareholder-value-focused decisions that we have now, he may have acted differently.

But he didn't. So he didn't.

While the Business Roundtable inserted community, employees, and the planet into a corporation's redefined purpose, the long-term results that Jack (and others like him) generated told a different story.

We didn't have to abandon shareholder primacy because it was bad for the planet. We had to abandon shareholder primacy because it was bad for business.

Jack was CEO of General Electric (GE) from 1981 to 2001. He had a relentless focus on maximizing shareholder value and accomplished it through aggressive cost-cutting, layoffs, and financial engineering while neglecting investments in innovation and long-term sustainability. As David Gelles notes in his book *The Man Who Broke Capitalism*, "Welch's GE was a masterclass in how to create the illusion of prosperity."

With the benefit of seeing how it all played out over time, we see that Welch's approach was short-sighted and ultimately detrimental to GE's long-term health. As Roger Martin has said, "Those who were exclusively focused on driving shareholder value didn't."

After Welch's retirement, GE began to unravel. In 2018, GE was removed from the Dow Jones, a symbolic fall from grace for a once-mighty powerhouse. Clearly, the obsession with shareholder value led to a focus on short-term profits at the expense of long-term investment, innovation, and growth.

Short-term thinking can lead to long-term failure.

The current pursuit of purpose is a direct response to the shortcomings of the shareholder primacy era. By focusing on purpose, companies can focus their thinking, create stronger relationships with and better experiences for important stakeholders, and ultimately drive sustainable growth.

Contrary to what I used to believe, I don't think Jack was evil. I think he was brilliant. But with the benefit of hindsight, his tenure and everything that followed carries an important reminder:

> **Short-term thinking can lead to long-term failure.**

But you know what else can lead to long-term failure? Pursuing the wrong type of purpose.

The Purpose Hail Mary

Amid all the issues, all the hate, and all the pressure that came with a new business era, leaders found themselves drowning in a sea of guilt and existential dread. They needed to change, but hey, Timmy had T-ball at six and the board needed the numbers by eight.

So, they did what any self-respecting capitalist would do: They pretended to care.

They churned out purpose statements so earnest and heartwarming, they could make a grown man weep. They promised to save the planet, foster equality, and generally make the world a better place. It was a masterclass in corporate virtue signaling and superficial solutions.

And the beautifully written purpose statements weren't only empty promises, they were completely divorced from the actual business of these companies.

Did you know that Philip Morris International—yes, *that* Philip Morris—has a purpose statement? It's "Building a better tomorrow." Go back and read that again.

Philip Morris makes their money by selling cigarettes.

It's not just that they're not living up to their purpose, it's that their purpose has absolutely nothing to do with what they do. It's like a bakery claiming to be dedicated to "promoting world peace through interpretive dance" while only selling $500 cupcakes to the elite.

In a bizarre twist that could only come from people who work in bathing suits, *Sports Illustrated* Swimsuit created a platform, Pay with Change, in 2022. It wanted to celebrate companies that were creating positive change for women, right within the pages of *SI*'s famous swimsuit issue. They also committed to investing a percentage of every ad dollar into the *Sports Illustrated* Gender Equity Fund, which supports nonprofits dedicated to creating an equitable future for all women.

MJ Day, editor in chief of *SI* Swimsuit, explained, "It's not just about showcasing beauty anymore; it's about changing the narrative."

Come again?

For decades, the swimsuit issue has been synonymous with objectifying women. Is it just me or does the sudden creation of a platform promoting gender equity feel like a desperate attempt to stay relevant?

Look, I may be wrong here, but isn't it too little, too late? Is the sound you hear the collective sigh from across the nation? I'm sure millions looked to the sky and thought, "Come on."

Dawn Hawkins, executive director of the National Center on Sexual Exploitation, accompanied her eye roll with a more pointed statement:

> As per usual, *SI*'s reductionist version of "female empowerment" perpetuates the message that women exist as mere props for male sexual fantasies.

Sounds like a little "purpose pushback." And it's in full gear.

As Chris Rock so brilliantly put it in his Netflix special *Selective Outrage,*

> Every business is full of shit... They don't even tell you about the product anymore. They just tell you how much charity they do.

Rock then took aim at Lululemon, the $100-yoga-pants purveyors who proudly proclaim they don't support racism, sexism, or hate. His response?

> Who gives a fuck? You're just selling yoga pants... Most people would prefer $20 racist yoga pants.

Savage, but he's got a point.

We've all witnessed the rainbow-washing during Pride Month, the performative allyship during Black Lives Matter, and countless other examples of corporate virtue signaling.

In a recent article for *Strategy* magazine, Will Novosedlik dug into the issues. He highlighted how the relentless march toward purpose has led some companies astray. Unilever, once lauded for its sustainable living plan under former CEO Paul Polman, started facing investor backlash when it seemed that purpose had overtaken profitability. By October 2023, Unilever's newest CEO, Hein Schumacher, admitted that the company had been guilty of "force-fitting" purpose into its brands, detracting from actual business growth.

Business leaders got purpose wrong.
And consumers are getting tired of the platitudes.

It's time to embrace the *real* purpose era—
where purpose guides you, it doesn't blindfold you.
I know that a focus on shareholder primacy can limit the long-term growth of an organization. But so can an overreaction that prioritizes cause over corporate.
Yes, we should treat our employees with respect and dignity and provide an amazing frictionless experience for them to work in. Yes, we should do it because we're good human beings. But we should also do it because we're good business leaders. Delivering an amazing experience to people you depend on to deliver an amazing experience is simply good for business.

The world pushed business leaders into adopting and embracing purpose.
Far too many got it wrong.

Should businesses work to save the planet?
Of course they should.
But saving the planet isn't a purpose.
It's an expectation.

Should businesses work to increase
the diversity of their teams?
Of course they should.
But diversity isn't a purpose.
It's an expectation.

Should businesses care about their employees and
suppliers and the communities in which they operate?
Of course they should.
But caring for the community isn't a purpose.
It's an expectation.

Should businesses be promoting gender equality
and ensuring that women break through the
glass ceiling that has existed for far too long?
Of course they should. But equality isn't a purpose.
It's an expectation.

Corporate purpose is strategically linked
to where you make your money.
It is a higher-order belief that inspires *why*
you do what you do. Not *how* you do it.

All those things are, as Rotman School
of Business told us, "business now."
They're not unimportant. They're expected.

Let's not throw the purpose baby out with the ethically sourced bathwater.

A purpose statement should be the strategic heart of the organization.

With the very mention of "drive," GM's purpose, "We stand together to drive the world forward," is strategically linked to where they make their money. It is a purpose that serves their commercial needs *and* their moral needs.

Purpose should guide growth.
But it won't and it can't if it's not connected to all the things you need to grow.

Welcome to the Real Purpose Era

Leaders overreacted, got purpose wrong, and sparked the justifiable backlash.

But hey, let's not throw the purpose baby out with the ethically sourced bathwater. Real purpose is not only a priority; it's defining the era of modern business we're deep in the middle of.

Roger Martin has done a ton of work in this area, and I encourage you to check it out. In my opinion, he's one of the best business minds we have. Modern business has evolved through three distinct eras: the manager era, the shareholder primacy era, and the purpose era.

The Manager Era

The manager era marked the shift from owner-operated businesses to professionally run businesses. It's when plumbers realized that they may be experts in plumbing, but they aren't experts in business. They wanted to grow their businesses so they turned to trained managers and MBAs to do it.

The Shareholder Primacy Era

At some point, the owner looked around and realized that the managers were making all the money. What's the point of starting your own business if you're going to turn over the riches to someone who hasn't taken the risk to get there?

Enter the shareholder primacy era, when owners and shareholders were the priority. If anyone was going to get paid, it was the people who bought in, not the ones who came along for the ride. But as I pointed out earlier, those who had exclusively focused on driving shareholder value didn't. And even if they did, they certainly didn't outperform their peers.

In his book *Fixing the Game*, Roger Martin states,

> Our theories of shareholder value maximization and stock-based compensation have the ability to destroy our economy and rot out the core of American capitalism... We must shift the focus of companies back to the customer and away from shareholder value... The current theory holds that the singular goal of the corporation should be shareholder value maximization. Instead, companies should place customers at the center of the firm and focus on delighting them, while earning an acceptable return for shareholders.

And that sets up the era we're currently in.

The Purpose Era

The answer, of course, lies in purpose.

When organizations can articulate why they exist through purpose, they can get a clear sense of direction, and they can better connect their employees to the organization, provide more fulfilling employment, deliver amazing experiences, and generate personal and organizational growth.

Important to note and reiterate: In this era, social causes as a proxy for purpose should not be mistaken for the fundamental reason a company exists. The causes should be a critical part of how the business operates (equitably, with inclusivity, sustainably), not why the business operates in the first place.

When an organization focuses on purpose and executing against purpose, guess what they generate? Shareholder value. It's a by-product of purpose-focused decisions, not the goal itself.

The real purpose era is about aligning your actions with your beliefs, not contorting your beliefs to fit your actions.

What do you believe? And how will that focus your actions to drive growth?

The Brand Belief

In addition to owning Church+State and writing books, I travel all over and use my comedy skills, my advertising experience, my outside observer insights, and my content creation process to add value and entertainment to organizations, associations, and more. I really enjoy it.

I love the energy of the room, the intimate interactions with audience members, and the challenge of generating insights for a different category and organization every time out. Besides, who doesn't enjoy doing a job and getting an immediate evaluation of your effort as soon as you finish?

I am a keynote speaker. Until I wasn't. Because I couldn't.

I defined myself by what I did, and when I was prevented from doing it for 15 months in 2020 and '21, I initially struggled to define myself. I was a speaker, but speakers are usually people who stand onstage, in person, and deliver material in front of a live audience. I may have had different SKUs, but I had one product: in-person speaking.

What does a keynote speaker do when they can't be a keynote speaker anymore? Like Bo Burnham, I reconnected with my fundamental beliefs about why I do what I do. And when I started to explore that, I realized it had nothing to do with the superficial things I got from it. My real satisfaction didn't come from the laughs; it came from the silence that followed the laughs—when people were thinking about what I said, instead of laughing at what I said.

I believe that everyone wants to do the right thing at work. They're just not sure what the right thing is. And helping people think through that didn't require me to be onstage. I could (and did) do it with books, podcasts, agency clients, articles, and more LinkedIn posts than any one person should attach their name to.

My question changed from "What am I going to do?" to "How can I help people figure out what to do?" Hello, personal growth. Nice to meet ya.

It was a powerful lesson for me. If you define yourself or your organization by what you do, and what you do needs to change, how do you move forward?

The definition of what each of us does is constantly evolving. But the reason why we do it shouldn't.

Now, purpose may be the strategic heartbeat of your business and critical to guiding personal growth, but you first have to articulate what it is. And that can be a painful exercise filled with strategy consultants, flip charts, stakeholder interviews, groupthink, and more buzzwords than a game of buzzword bingo.

About a third of our business at Church+State is strategy work, and much of it hinges on aligning the necessary inputs and perspectives to land on a purpose that informs and inspires behaviors inside and outside an organization.

I keep using the term "purpose," but—ironically, given the title of this book—at Church+State we use the term "Brand Belief" instead. "Purpose" has some baggage, and it means a hundred different things to a hundred different people. Brand Belief is a bit more ownable, too. It's different from mission, vision, North Star, purpose, BHAG, and any other term in corporate ethics clutter. We think it gets to the core of what really matters, too.

It answers one simple question:

> **What does this organization fundamentally believe?**

It's not an easy question to answer, and it shouldn't be. But the answer is the foundation that supports everything you do and the strategic thread that runs through it all.

We just finish the statement: We believe that...

It may look like three dots there, but those three dots can take months of work, tons of consultation, and multiple drafts before everyone in the room nods in agreement.

If you're Airbnb, do you believe that people should rent out their spare room? No. You believe that people should feel like they belong anywhere. Tied to where they make their money but elected above it.

Does Axe Body Spray believe that young men should bathe in deodorant? No. They believe that men should celebrate their individuality and be as attractive as they can be.

Does Google believe that people should be able to say, "Hey Google, is it raining outside?" from anywhere in their house? No. They believe that information empowers everyone.

Does IKEA believe that furniture should be difficult to pronounce and assembled exclusively by Allen keys? No. They believe that everyday life should be better.

Does Disney believe that life's experiences are worth lining up for? No. They believe that storytelling can entertain, inform, and inspire people.

Does Nike believe that we should win everything we compete in? No. They believe that everyone's an athlete.

Does Walmart believe that people should be able to buy roast beef, khakis, and prescriptions in the same place? No. They believe that people live better when they save money.

What do you believe? And more importantly, how can it focus your growth?

No Traveling Allowed

What you don't know by reading this is that behind this book is a gargantuan man who stands six-foot-ten... give or take a foot and a half. Okay, I may not be a towering presence on the court, and basketball isn't really a game that I'm an expert in, but I know one thing about basketball that's relevant to our discussion: When you're dribbling down the court and come to a stop, you can't start moving again and resume your path down the court. That's traveling, and traveling is not allowed in basketball.

Purpose
is your
pivot foot.

The one thing you can do is pivot on your foot.

In James Naismith's game, the pivot foot is the foot that a player keeps planted on the floor when they have possession of the ball and are not dribbling. It acts as an anchor and allows the player to rotate their body while maintaining control of the ball—without traveling. Once a player establishes a pivot foot, they can lift their other foot and move it in any direction, as long as the pivot foot remains in contact with the floor in the same spot.

It may be anchored, but the pivot foot is what enables players to change direction, fake out defenders, and, most importantly for our discussion here, create scoring opportunities. They don't call it "growth," but I will.

Well, purpose is your pivot foot.

It keeps you grounded and focused while simultaneously giving you the freedom to explore new directions and new possibilities for growth. You can rotate, find new angles, look for opportunities, and explore what your next move will be—but you're doing it from that one focused spot on the floor.

Purpose is what ensures you don't end up running all over the place. Without purpose, you risk committing leadership traveling—engaging in random activities, chasing unproven tactics, and running around your court of play exploring half-baked ideas that are without merit or foundation.

THE PURPOSE OF PURPOSE

Netflix didn't start out making original content. They were in the DVD rental business. But their purpose wasn't tied to DVDs; it was tied to providing convenient entertainment. When they were looking to grow, they didn't run around selling Rollerblades. Their purpose was their pivot foot to explore new directions, integrate new technology, and create a new and convenient entertainment product.

Your pivot foot doesn't just keep you from traveling on the court.

It prevents your employees from feeling lost in the game.

From Engaged to Energized

What is happiness? That question might sound like it belongs in a late-night dorm room debate surrounded by bongs with the Grateful Dead playing in the background.

That being said, happiness is the only metric that really matters in our lives. If you're successful but not happy, what's the point?

So, what does happiness come down to? Well, in my career and in my life, it has really been about three key elements: enjoyment, satisfaction, and, you guessed it, purpose. My good friend Neil Pasricha explored the topic in much more depth in *The Happiness Equation*. Neil has nine secrets to happiness, and his thinking has helped me out a lot.

Enjoyment comes from those moments that bring us joy. For me, it's things like spending cuddly time with my kids reading before bed. It's going to see a Blue Jays game with a good friend. It's sitting on the roof of our boat house with a glass of scotch as the sun goes down across the lake. Ahhhhh, my resting heart rate just dropped thinking about it. While financial success can enable those moments, it can rarely create those moments.

Satisfaction, on the other hand, is that deep sense of accomplishment we feel when we achieve a goal. You can guess how satisfied I was when I finished writing this book. But I also had micro-levels of satisfaction after every sentence, paragraph, and chapter. Satisfaction requires effort expended to fulfill a goal. There's challenge involved, and sometimes happiness doesn't show up until the end. Satisfaction sounds like it's reached through a solo effort, but team satisfaction is just as worthwhile and can, in my experience, deliver even more happiness because of the additional challenge that comes with working with other people. Not only do you have to win the pitch, but you also have to bypass egos, coordinate efforts, and compromise with your own team.

And purpose? Purpose is how our lives gain meaning. It ensures that what we do matters—not just to ourselves but to the world around us. Do you know how many times I've heard people in advertising ask, "What the hell are we doing here?"

As I thought about this, I thought I would turn to Fishbowl, the professional platform that functions as a virtual watercooler for employees across various industries. Normally, I stay away from any platform where people can be anonymous. I can appreciate that people need a safe place to complain about their bosses or the industry without getting penalized for their thoughts, but just because I think it should exist doesn't mean I want to engage with it or support it. That being said, I wanted to see if anybody was complaining about the advertising industry while working in the advertising industry. And within five seconds, there it was.

A person only identified as "creative" asked:

> **Do you regret getting into advertising? Like, deep down? None of that "oh you get paid to be creative" shit.**

The comments gave interesting perspectives. From an associate creative director:

> I teeter on two thoughts. Sometimes I feel like I've gamed the system of life whenever I read how bad people are struggling out there with cost of living, etc. I managed to work a job that's pretty fun, fairly easy, and pays well. On the other hand... sometimes I think about how many insanely talented hardworking people are in meetings discussing the dumbest shit possible and think damn wish we were talking about solving some real problems. Not discussing how to fix some blueberry bouncing off a waffle the wrong way in post.

A senior copywriter balanced it out:

> Happy! My life would be substantially worse if I went to law school intead [*sic*].

But others brought us back to a depressing reality:

> Maybe 10 years ago I would have said no, but now I kind of find myself a little bit jealous of, like, the dentist that's had the relative privilege of pulling up to the same boring old office every day for their entire career. (A vice president)

> This 100 percent. In your 20s this is the best job of all time. In your 30s and older you really start to question all your life decisions knowing you've never seen a single person in the industry willingly retire. The only thing waiting for you after advertising is another career or poverty. (A strategy director)

A line that is often used in advertising circles is "We're not saving lives, people."

We aren't. Until we do.

Just over the past few years, I've been lucky to be involved in some projects that have brought incredible fulfillment to our team. In Canada, we created the brand Talk Suicide, a national network of suicide prevention centers. We helped MediaSmarts stop misinformation during the pandemic. We've done strategy and creative for people like UNICEF, Action against Hunger, SickKids Foundation, Innovative Medicines Canada, and a whole host of other important organizations. And we've helped all the for-profit organizations communicate effectively so that they can bring happiness and fulfillment to other people.

Our Brand Belief is "We believe people used to vote with their wallets, but now they vote with their time. So, we create stuff that's worthy of their attention." Of course, we don't always get it right and not everything we create is worthy of a customer's time, but when we do hit it out of the park, regardless of who the client is, it's really meaningful.

For me, that's more fulfilling than most other careers out there.

While we work with Google now, I have had the opportunity to work with most parts of Microsoft over the years as a creative director on their business.

Microsoft has put forward a powerful example of how purpose can transform the workplace. Instead of focusing solely on employee "engagement," a metric that has been the go-to for HR pros for years, they shifted their focus to employee "thriving."

Engagement alone doesn't capture the full picture of employee well-being. You can be engaged in your work but still feel drained, unfulfilled, or disconnected from the larger purpose of the organization. When you're engaged but disconnected, exhaustion and bitterness can set in as you ponder the "What does it all mean?" questions.

Microsoft defines thriving as being "energized and empowered to do meaningful work." And let's be honest, meaningful work is when growth occurs. Growth doesn't occur when you're doing all that low-calorie work that seems to fill most of our days—trying to empty your inbox, hopping on quick and responsive virtual calls, filling out mundane paperwork, and other mindless tasks.

Growth occurs when you do meaningful and important work that will change the trajectory of your business.

Look, employees need more than just a paycheck, perks, and pizza to be happy at work. They need to feel that their work is meaningful, that it adds value not only to the company but also to their own sense of self-worth and to society.

When employees understand what their organization believes in *and* they clearly see their valued and respected roles in bringing it to life and are empowered to do it, they find great meaning. They don't put in the hours, check the boxes, and fill their days. They thrive.

When they constantly learn and are challenged in completing those responsibilities, it's an investment in their personal growth. Would you look at that: When their personal growth is tied to the purpose of the organization, we see a direct line from personal growth to organizational growth. When you know you've made a difference, you'll work differently.

That's what I call alignment. They thrive. You thrive. We all thrive.

But without a direct link to a shared purpose, all employees risk going rogue and pursuing their own paths, their own ways, which dilutes the impact of the organization.

Happiness is a journey, not a destination. And in the workplace, your Brand Belief or purpose is the map that keeps everyone moving toward growth.

THE RUNNER
SAVANNAH BANANAS

FOCUSED BY PURPOSE

You'd think that a baseball team would have a purpose tied to baseball, wouldn't you? You know, something that includes words like "home run," "victory," or "battah-battah-battah."

Nope. Not here. Remember, growth wasn't going to come from the game. It was going to come from the experience. Jesse Cole wasn't inspired by George Steinbrenner, Arte Moreno, or any other baseball team owner. He was inspired by Walt Disney.

As Andrew Lock, author of *Walt Disney's Way*, said,

> **With inspiration from both P.T. Barnum and Walt Disney, Jesse reminds us that anything is possible when you're willing to reject industry norms and literally do the opposite of what most businesses do.**

For me, the key part in Andrew's description is "willing to reject industry norms." That bold attitude of not being satisfied with what has always been done is the exact sentiment in the Brand Belief of the Savannah Bananas.

> **We believe there's a better way to do almost everything.**

It's strategically connected to what they do. But it goes well beyond what they do. It takes them from product (baseball) to purpose (belief). It can work for the product on the field—every hitter and pitcher should be striving for continuous improvement. But it can also affect the experience in the ballpark and every department in the organization. There are industry norms for every aspect of the company, and their purpose inspires them to reject those norms to find the better way to do it.

Marketing. Sales. HR. Finance. There are better ways to do all of it.

In the end, the Bananas' Brand Belief wasn't just a catchy slogan. It was the catalyst for every action they took and every decision they made to pursue growth.

Did the Bananas split? What did they do?
Read about it at the end of the next chapter.

"If you don't know IYKYK means 'If you know, you know,' your consumers know something you don't know, you know?"

PABLO PICASSO

DEFINED BY YOUR ACTIONS
(THE DO PART)

Purpose without action is a useless purpose.

Do It on Purpose

My very first cell phone provider was a company called Clearnet Communications. I won't give you the year, but know that it involved rubbing sticks together to communicate a message across cell towers.

In 2000, Clearnet was acquired by Telus.

In an interesting move, when Telus acquired Clearnet, they didn't swallow every part of the company. Recognizing the strength of Clearnet's brand, Telus abandoned their own brief legacy and adopted Clearnet's brand assets into the new Telus brand. It was the right move. Clearnet's bold and contemporary design, use of bright greens and purples, and cute animal imagery differentiated Telus from the big and boring telcos in the market. Its tagline summed it all up: "The future is friendly."

I always felt the line "The future is friendly" was an inspiring statement, but it offered no hint of what Telus did to make it happen. There was a disconnect between the promised utopia of the future and who was doing what to get us there.

In early 2021, Telus must have felt their ears burning, because they evolved the tagline from "The future is friendly" to "Let's make the future friendly."

It wasn't enough to believe that the future *could* be friendly or that the future *would* be friendly. Telus needed to remind us of the actions required to get there. The inclusion of "Let's" turned a statement into an invitation. "Let's make the future friendly" is a call to arms for customers, employees, and partners to join Telus in creating a better future.

Purpose without action is a useless purpose. Spending all your time writing one without allocating even more resources to generating the actions required to bring it to life is a waste of time. Growth won't happen because you wrote a purpose. It will happen when you align and prioritize actions to reinforce your purpose and growth.

Proclamations without participation won't drive growth.
Aspirations without action won't drive growth.
Pledges without performance won't drive growth.
Words without work won't drive growth.
Or in Telus's words, if you want your future to be friendly, you gotta do some stuff to make it happen.

But you can't just do it. You have to do it on purpose. Your friendly future isn't a given; it's a goal. And like any good goal, it takes a whole lot of purpose-fueled hustle to get there.

That's Not How We Do It around Here

You walk into the boardroom. You're armed with the 53 slides you tweaked right up until the moment you got in the elevator.

You've done your research.

You pulled the data.

You got quotes and testimonials and initial buy-in from all the people around you.

You set the stage with your up-front thoughts.

You use your best stage voice and rehearsed jokes to get their attention and keep their attention.

And as you approach your strategic crescendo with confidence and poise, you click to reveal your bold and insightful recommendations.

That's when the wind gets taken out of your sales.

Gary, the head of sales, or Barb, the head of finance, or Kelli, the head of procurement, or Anthony, the head of complaining... it doesn't matter who it is. The only thing that matters is that they've been in the organization longer than you have, and they use their body language as a force that rivals most Marvel characters.

It starts with the folding of the arms. They look to the fluorescent lights and sigh. Since they went to that one seminar on giving feedback, they begin with something positive like "I really like the color palette of your presentation" or "That blouse really pops against the prison-like off-white walls of the boardroom." They pause, and their mind searches while their face says, "How do I elevate my status in this meeting without sounding like a total jerk?"

And then they just default to their usual corporate jab:

> **These ideas sound great but...**
> **that's not how we do it around here.**

Ah, the eight deadly words of any organization.
That's not how we do it around here.
They are the ultimate buzzkill for innovation and the archnemesis of progress.

Look, if everything was peachy and perfect, we wouldn't be talking about change in the first place, right? Clearly, you want to grow, and growth isn't happening. If it was, you'd probably be focused on trying to contain it.

When someone pulls out this line, what they're really saying is "That's not how *I* want to do it around here." Translation? "I'm comfortable, I'm settled, and frankly, I'd like to keep my job without rocking the boat, thank you very much."

But here's the thing: Growth doesn't care about anyone's comfort zone. As the title of my friend and fellow speaker Billy Anderson's book put it: Your comfort zone is killing you.

Growth isn't interested in maintaining the status quo.

Typically, the people suggesting something new aren't trying to mess with tradition just to be difficult. They see something others don't: a gap in the onboarding process, a flaw in the invoicing system, or a fresh way to meet your numbers.

Their biggest rivals are the TNHWDIAH (that's not how we do it around here) people. Those people aren't interested in having their own Bo Burnham moment. They're interested in survival. What they don't realize is that growth *is* survival. Without it, the organization's days, not to mention theirs, are numbered.

So, what's the antidote to this stubborn resistance? It's not banging your head against the wall or scheduling another meeting before the meeting.

It's purpose.

Purpose is the secret sauce that can turn even the most change-averse person into an active and willing participant, wearing the T-shirt, rallying those around them and leading the charge.

When you align change with a clear, compelling purpose, suddenly it's not about tweaking someone's daily grind—it's about moving the organization toward something bigger, something better.

Purpose makes it harder for people to dig in their heels and say, "No thanks, I'm good." It's easier to build alignment around a shared vision than it is to sell them on a random growth model you sketched out on a whiteboard. Purpose gets everyone on the same page, clears up any suspicion about motives, and gives people a reason to buy in.

So, next time someone drops the "That's not how we do it around here" bomb, lead with purpose—and with the words that have been attributed to Thomas Jefferson:

> **If you want something you've never had,
> you must be willing to do something you've never done.**

Your actions should echo your purpose so loudly that words become redundant.

The Essential Do

Sailing wasn't a top activity in the south end of Oshawa, so I've never really sailed—other than that one time at camp. And that didn't end well. Apparently, the boom can hit your head, and "boom" isn't the noise it creates.

Still, I have had the pleasure of speaking to US Sailing several times over the past decade. They're a wonderful group. I last addressed them in 2024. They had a new CEO, a reinvigorated board, and a membership base that had navigated both fun and challenging times during the pandemic.

For most of you, tracking sales is the primary metric of success. But for sport governing bodies, it's the level of interest in the sport. Increase interest and you get more participants, better clubs, higher revenue, and stronger competition.

As you start your purpose-focused growth journey, you can learn from US Sailing. Your purpose can focus your actions, but how you define what you do either embraces growth or limits growth.

For US Sailing, this meant asking, "What exactly is defined as sailing?"

I know, I know, this sounds just as ridiculous as if you asked, "What exactly do we do here?" in your company.

But it's still important to ensure your growth is the right kind of growth.

Is windsurfing sailing?
Is kiteboarding sailing?
Is dinghy-sailing sailing?
Is sailing exclusively defined by a traditional view of larger boats?
Is it me with an unbuttoned shirt flapping in the wind riding a giant inflatable unicorn considered sailing or just a poor decision that led to ridicule from my cottage neighbors?

The debate between traditionalists and forward-thinkers is crucial, but it's the answer to these questions that will either open doors to growth or limit the organization's potential.

This is where purpose becomes so important. Purpose creates a belief behind what you do *and* it informs what you do.

But before you can start changing what you do to drive growth, you need to be crystal clear about what it is you do in the first place. How can you support and extend your core business if people aren't aligned on what the core action of the organization is?

I told the US Sailing audience, "Purpose isn't about the specific type of wind-powered vessel you use; it's about the joy and experience of being on the water when you don't have a motor propelling you forward."

My take on what their purpose should be:

"We believe that everyone should sail through life."

That's a Brand Belief that can set up tremendous growth, but it's useless unless they define what they specifically do to reinforce it.

I completed my thinking with an Essential Do.

"We believe that everyone should sail through life *so* we encourage sailing participation and excellence through education, competition, and equal opportunity."

We believe *this*.
So, we do *this*.
What they believe is
directly linked to what they do.

How you define what you do allows you to embrace growth or it limits it.

The bridge between them is "so."

Your organization believes in something, *so* you produce a product that reinforces that belief.

Remember our Brand Belief examples? Here they are paired with an Essential Do.

Airbnb: We believe that people should feel like they belong anywhere, *so* we connect travelers with accommodations where they can feel like they're part of the community.

Axe Body Spray: We believe that guys should celebrate their individuality and be as attractive as they can be, *so* we make products that help guys be attractive and confident.

Google: We believe that information empowers everyone, *so* we organize the world's information to be useful and universally accessible.

IKEA: We believe that everyday life should be better, *so* we create well-designed, functional home furnishings at prices *so* low that as many people as possible can afford them.

Disney: We believe storytelling can entertain, inform, and inspire people, *so* we create magical experiences that bring stories to life and spark imagination in people of all ages.

Nike: We believe that everyone's an athlete, *so* we create the best apparel and equipment to help them perform at their best.

Walmart: We believe that people live better when they save money, *so* we offer products at the lowest possible prices every single day.

They think, *so* they do. And so should you.

As an organization determines its growth strategies, the natural question to ask after articulating an Essential Do is "What else could we do?"

When Airbnb asked themselves that question, their purpose guided their growth.

When refugees were fleeing Ukraine, a cofounder of Airbnb shared this out to socials: "Airbnb and airbnb.org are working with our hosts to house up to 100,000 refugees fleeing from Ukraine for free."

Why did they *do* that?

Because they believe that people should feel like they belong anywhere. They primarily connect travelers with accommodations where they can feel like they're part of the community. But what else should they do to drive growth?

Well, philanthropic efforts are an interesting place to start. Saving people isn't their purpose, but their purpose allows them to save people.

What Else Can You Do?

You and your growth will be defined by the actions you take. But what should they be? It's a pretty big leap to go from "This is what you believe so this is what you do" to "Now go and do a bunch of other stuff, wave your wand, and growth will occur right before your eyes."

While there are many things you could do, undeniably, there is one that you need to do:

> **Focus on creating experiences people can't ignore.**

Whether it's for your customers, your prospects, your employees, or your partners, an amazing experience is the result of focusing on actions tied to purpose.

You don't improve your systems because you want to show you can. You do it to create an efficient and enjoyable experience for your team and customers. You don't improve marketing to get press. You do it to create a better experience for the prospects you're trying to acquire. You don't improve your culture for hugs and high fives. You improve culture because it creates a more fulfilling employee experience.

Better customer experience leads to growth.
Better employee experience leads to growth.
Better prospect experience leads to growth.

To lead yourself to growth, focus on experiences.

To lead yourself to growth, focus on experiences—personalized and frictionless experiences both inside and outside your organization.

What's Experience Anyhow?

When the Canada-US border opened after the pandemic restrictions and I returned to travel, my first gig was at the Bellagio in Las Vegas. Nothing like going back into the belly of the beast, huh? I was nervous about the prospect of travel and giddy at the thought of getting onstage again. I was also going to get to see some wonderful and talented friends from the speaking world, including Neen James, Mike Ganino, and Erin King.

But all that excitement quickly gave way to confusion and panic once I tried to figure out what it took to get back into the country. Different tests, different requirements, different timelines, and different procedures. If I got it right, I'd get to go home. If I got it wrong, I was going to be camped out in Vegas being woken by the ding-dings of slot machines and the rowdiness of bachelor parties.

I thought a testing facility was on-site at the hotel, but I was wrong. The result? I was sprinting to get a PCR test so I could go home. I took an Uber to a testing site on my way to the airport and then waited in sheer panic until the results arrived just in time, right before I boarded.

It was in that moment, sweating and panting through the mask on my face, that I heard about Switch Health. They leverage technology to provide convenient and accessible healthcare solutions... like PCR tests.

I heard about Switch Health through Aeroplan, Air Canada's loyalty mileage program. As soon as I got home, I dug in. Here's how it worked.

I ordered a bunch of PCR testing kits from Switch Health, and they arrived in the mail within a day or two. I took one kit with me on my next trip across the border (to Vegas again). On the day of my return flight, I engaged in a virtual video call with a health practitioner, who verified my identity and witnessed me collecting my own saliva and nasal swab samples. Once the test was complete, I inserted the sample into the testing device, which used RT-LAMP technology to analyze the sample for the presence of COVID-19 viral RNA.

I sent a picture of my results to Switch Health. The QR code sticker on the device linked the test results to my personal account. With my negative result, I received documentation to show the airline and customs officials.

I never tested positive, but I know that those results were automatically reported to public health authorities for contact tracing purposes.

Now *that* was an experience. Let's break down why.

First, it started with Aeroplan. Their clients encountered a problem—PCR testing confusion and panic—that they couldn't solve themselves. So, Aeroplan vetted those who could and promoted, introduced, and connected their clients to them. No searching. No questions of trust. I didn't know Switch Heath. But I knew (and trusted) Aeroplan.

Switch Health's online experience was simple and intuitive. I was able to order quickly and efficiently. And when the testing kits arrived at my home ahead of schedule, it was clear that the digital team worked seamlessly with the fulfillment team including—I'm assuming—a third-party courier service.

Once, I didn't realize I had used all my kits and desperately needed one on a Sunday night for a Monday morning departure. Ordering and receiving in that time frame was impossible. Luckily, Switch Health had a vending machine, publicly available 10 minutes from my house.

I was impressed with Switch Health's technology, impressed with the speed, impressed with the simplicity of the instructions, impressed with the tone of the health practitioner, and most importantly, I was impressed that it was impossible to cheat the system. Not only was it easy and convenient, it was legit.

Through it all, the experience wasn't one thing.
It was everything.
The introduction was part of a great experience.
The UX was part of a great experience.
The fulfillment was part of a great experience.
The technology was part of a great experience.
The people were part of a great experience.
The speed and efficiency were part of a great experience.

Every department and division was informed and inspired to work together to deliver on the purpose of the organization, and they were part of a great experience.

I went from a departure experience that was filled with panic, frustration, and fear that I was an idiot for getting it wrong to one where I felt confident, happy, and proud that I was informed enough to know about it. And I felt all of that from the comfort of my hotel room.

With so much ink on experience, you'd think there would be an acceptable and shared definition of it. I don't think there is. So, here's mine:

> **Experience is the sum of all the emotions generated by interactions that shapes an individual's relationship with a brand or organization.**

It's emotional.

It's generated by all interactions—the product, the process, and the people.

And it has a profound impact on how I see the brand in my life moving forward.

With Switch Health, every emotion at every interaction was positive, and each one countered an equal and opposite preexisting negative emotion. It was a total experience that featured deliberate connections between CX, EX, and UX.

But me saying that you should deliver an amazing experience is lazy. It's too complicated, has too many moving parts, and can't be covered in this book alone. Sure, *wow* moments capture attention, but you create lasting loyalty, develop trust, and keep customers coming back for more with personalized, frictionless experiences delivered by engaged employees.

I'm going to dive into those three aspects one by one: the personalized experience, the frictionless experience, and the employee experience.

THE PERSONALIZED EXPERIENCE

Retirement? Hell no. I need a minivan and wipes.

WHEN THE CHARACTER Norm Peterson entered the bar in *Cheers*, he would typically announce his arrival with "Afternoon, everybody." Everyone would yell "Norm!" And then Sam would say something like:

> SAM: What's shaking, Norm?
> NORM: All four cheeks and a couple of chins.

Norm's responses were worth waiting for. But so was the service. Like Norm, Cliff, and the gang, people want to go to a place where everybody knows them.

Part of a truly great experience is customized and personalized to the individual. Customers know what's possible, and they expect interactions that feel uniquely tailored to them. Whether it's personalized recommendations or a custom shopping experience or more, successful brands essentially say,

> I get you. I got you.

Identify Them

Our desire to be seen as unique human beings might be more pronounced now than it ever has been.

Maybe it's because we're bombarded by inappropriate sales pitches all the time. Maybe it's because of generational differences. Maybe it's because our digital behaviors have made us more insular, spending more time alone, forcing us to place greater importance on who we are as individuals. But more than any of that, there are more people busting out of the standard definitions of who we're expected to be.

At the time of writing, I'm a 54-year-old man with two children, both boys, four and six years old. I'm no Hugh Hefner, but I know I'm an old dad.

A little while ago, I took our kids to a drop-in art center for some painting, crafting, and artistic expression. The kids had been a bunch of times, but my wife was the one who had always dropped them off. So, when I showed up, one of the instructors welcomed us with "Max! Benny! Great to see you."

And then she turned to me. "Ahhhhh, you must be the grandpa..."

"Nope."

She froze, died a little inside, and stammered and clambered to find the words that would justify her embarrassment. I felt for her in that moment. She did nothing wrong.

Now, it's one thing for a person with only physical information to make an honest mistake. It's quite another for a business with access to formal and informal data to get it wrong. I get so many pitches based solely on my age that assume I'm just like everyone else.

"Hey, it looks like it's time to start converting your retirement savings..."

Retirement? Hell no. I need a minivan and wipes. (The wipes are for me.)

I'm a unique person with unique circumstances that create unique needs and unique problems that need to be solved. My frictions are nothing like the expected frictions of a 54-year-old.

Still, when it comes to expressing my true self, it's not like I've faced trauma, struggled with defining who I am, or overcome great societal barriers to be who I am. I can only imagine how frustrated someone who fought and clawed their way to be who they are must get when businesses get them wrong.

On the flip side, they must also feel so ecstatic when a business gets it right.

The challenge for all of us is that personalization is more complex than it has ever been.

The first personalization ever recorded probably went something like this:

> MERCHANT: You're William, right?
> WILLIAM: Yep. But you can call me Bill.
> MERCHANT: Nice to meet you, Bill.

Personalization was about understanding the difference between our formal names and the names we wish to be addressed by. It's a tad more complex than that, but the spirit remains. But yes, it's way more complicated. Even between the time that I wrote *Think Do Say* and today, it has changed drastically. At that time, personalization focused on giving people the ability to source custom content based on interests. But now? The very fabric of gender and sexuality has changed.

I'm not minimizing anyone's struggles when I say this, and I hate when people use the phrase "I identify as..." as a joke, but that declaration says it all: "I identify as..." I may be 54, but I identify as a young father with a new family. Some of you may be known as an accountant, but you identify as an artist. And most importantly, some people may be known as "Rachel" but identify as "Rick."

We all identify as someone that represents who we are to our core. And often it's not the obvious choice.

Enter Mastercard's True Name card, a groundbreaking initiative that took personalization to a whole new level.

The card lets people, especially those who are trans or nonbinary, use the name they want on their credit card—even if it's not their legal name. I can only imagine how it would feel to pay for merchandise with a credit card that has the wrong name on it. And then have to explain myself to a merchant who suspected I was using someone else's card.

As one person said in the True Name launch video, "It's tough to have a reminder every single day of a name you've chosen to move away from. It's just a reminder of struggle and difficulty. I don't think I have anything with my name on it at this point. So thank you. I feel people are seeing me as myself now. Seeing and feeling the name is just so validating."

Now that's an experience that can lead to growth.

If a credit card can acknowledge someone for who they truly are, I'm sure we can.

When You Don't, and When You Do

When companies fail to personalize offerings, they risk alienating customers, reinforcing harmful biases, and missing out on substantial growth opportunities.

But let's say you're too busy. Or too tired, too confused, too bitter, or too closed-minded because you think it's a woke conspiracy. So you don't do it. No biggie, right?

Well, failing to personalize can lead to significant negative outcomes.

A consumer watchdog recently discovered that Canadian financial institutions, including banks and insurance companies, were found to be making inappropriate product recommendations based on racial stereotypes rather than genuinely understanding the unique needs and circumstances of individual customers. They found that things like overdraft protection and creditor insurance were more often recommended to Indigenous and racialized consumers.

That's right. They weren't just avoiding personalization; they were actively making recommendations based on generalizations. Kinda like coming to me and pitching retirement financial plans. Only worse.

Obviously, I'm not a bank hater. Around the world, financial institutions do very well and do some good while they do it. They're active in their communities and often use profits to fund organizations that try to solve the very problems they're apparently contributing to.

I know these acts of generalization weren't done by evil minds with evil intentions. Of course not. This example just highlights a dangerous pitfall: When you don't see the whole human being, the only thing you'll often see is a stereotype. How could you not? The banks didn't consider their customers' entire financial picture. Instead, they made assumptions based on the two-dimensional picture before them.

The result? Customers were offered products that didn't align with their real needs. That led to mistrust and dissatisfaction. It didn't just hurt the client; it damaged the relationship between the client and the bank, which—I'm assuming—led to missed opportunities for both.

True personalization is about more than knowing a customer's name or purchase history. It's the ability and the desire to see the whole human being. Do it and you'll create exceptional experiences that foster loyalty and build trust. Just remember—the benefits go beyond financial growth. The pursuit of personalization pushes teams to innovate, streamline operations to scale great ideas, and develop programs that bring meaning to their work. It's a catalyst for holistic growth, benefiting both the business and the people it serves. True personalization is a win-win: It's good for the balance sheet and good for the soul.

Acknowledge Them

From the 1950s until he retired in 2012, Jackie Mason built his comedy career on pointing out the humor in North American immigrant cultures. No one was left untouched. Italian. Irish. Polish. English. Scottish. German. Jewish. Jackie Mason made fun of everybody. Well, almost everybody.

The next wave of immigrants came from China, Vietnam, India, Pakistan, South and North Korea, and other countries in Asia. Who spoke for them, joked for them, and made fun of their rituals to help them laugh at themselves?

One of the first to do it was Russell Peters.

In an industry dominated by mass appeal and broad generalizations, Peters identified a rather large gap in the market: Asian immigrants. Their communities were growing rapidly and were largely ignored by mainstream comedians.

Instead of trying to appeal to the masses, speak directly to those who feel unseen.

As the son of Indian immigrants, Peters understood the nuances and challenges of living between two cultures. When he impersonated his Indian father saying "Somebody gonna get a hurt real bad," there were millions of people who knew exactly what he meant. He knew that the immigrant experience was rich with humor and completely absent on the world's biggest stages.

Rather than diluting his material to appeal to everyone, Peters doubled down on specific cultural references, accents, and stereotypes that spoke directly to the new immigrant experience.

He built a following. He built a business. In 2013, he was ranked the third highest-paid comedian in the world by *Forbes*, with earnings of $21 million that year.

Customizing and personalizing products that acknowledge a culture can help make inroads to communities that have been ignored by too many. Sounds like a great opportunity to grow as people and as a business.

Fenty Beauty's diverse foundation shades cater to a wide range of skin tones. Nike's Pro Hijab empowers Muslim women to participate in sports while honoring their religious beliefs. Halal food options are increasingly available in major grocery chains, acknowledging the dietary needs of Muslim communities. And as we saw earlier, companies like Mattel are diversifying their toy lines, introducing dolls that reflect a wider range of ethnicities and cultural backgrounds.

Even KitKat is getting in on the action. Of course, KitKat's belief "Everyone deserves a break" has always been central to their identity, but they supercharged it by launching the first-ever KitKat Iftar Bar, specifically tailored for the Muslim community during Ramadan.

KitKat recognized a significant cultural moment in the daily Iftar tradition during Ramadan and created a product that celebrated this break in a meaningful way.

Break. Break. Get it? They honored a sacred tradition with a special edition product that resonated deeply with the Muslim community.

Growth doesn't happen when you do the same things for the same people. Instead of desperately trying to appeal to the masses, you could speak directly to those who feel unseen.

So, in the spirit of Russell Peters and KitKat, let's stop trying to be everything to everyone. Let's create products and experiences that make people feel seen, heard, and understood.

Include Them

Apparently, my mom wasn't supposed to live past six years old.

She was born in 1936 and suffered from spina bifida, which develops in the first month of gestation when the spine and spinal cord don't form properly. In my mom's case, there was an opening in the spine, which exposed the spinal cord and the nerves that served her lower limbs and bladder.

Needless to say, the treatment in 1936 wasn't close to what it is today.

When she was a child, she had to have her left leg amputated. Her right foot was a clubfoot—a foot that is turned inward and downward and is rounder than a normal foot. She lived her life with crutches, braces, wheelchairs, and an overall lack of mobility and freedom. Her movement was slow, her range was short, and she needed help along the way. Because of her clubfoot, my mom never wore regular shoes. It's not like she could walk into a shoe store for a pair of Manolo Blahniks in size "club." Her right shoe was specially made to fit her foot in plain black leather. The left shoe for her prosthetic simply had to match it.

She never got to wear tennis shoes. She never got to wear cowboy boots. She never got to wear ballet slippers. And she never got to wear dress shoes. It wasn't until my mom was in her mid-50s that things changed. She met a pedorthist, someone trained in anatomy and biomechanics and specialized in designing and making orthopedic footwear.

He was the guy who made her shoes.

Inspired and curious, he asked my mom if she would be open to wearing a brace on her clubfoot. If made correctly, the brace could allow her to wear "normal" shoes. She went for it. Over a series of months, they tried and tested a number of different braces until they found one that worked. After more than 50 years of wearing the same type of shoes, my mom could go out and *shop* for shoes.

There was only one stipulation. Because the brace positioned her foot in a really unique way, she had to wear shoes with very strong ankle support. She didn't need three-inch heels. She needed basketball shoes.

Yes. My mom. A tiny and loud Italian and French woman in her mid-50s, who had never had the pleasure of wearing regular shoes, christened her newfound freedom with a pair of Air Jordans.

It was hilarious. And it was inspiring as hell.

I wish you could've seen the look on her face the first time she stood before us proudly wearing her new shoes. I wish you could've heard her talk about the shoes and her journey to get them with anyone who would listen. It was priceless.

I think my mom always felt like she was on the fringe of society. She couldn't do what everybody else did, and she couldn't wear what everybody else wore. But that day, she got to buy and wear the hottest ticket in town. She wore those Air Jordans to weddings, to reunions, to birthday parties, and more.

Finally, she was part of the team—not quite ready to dunk or shoot a three-pointer, but part of the team.

At its heart, I think personalization is about inclusion. We're finally getting around to including those who have been ignored or who have had one aspect of themselves ignored—their gender, their orientation, their marital status, their culture, their inability to read your website or hear your representative on a call, and more.

When companies tailor products and services for those with different abilities, they don't just improve the experience for a specific group; they create a ripple effect that enhances the experience for everyone.

Alphabet (Google's parent company) has done a wonderful job of making tech accessible for all. Live Caption automatically generates captions for videos and audio, making content more accessible for those who are deaf or hard of hearing. Lookout is an app that uses AI to assist people with no or low vision navigate their surroundings and identify objects. In Android, TalkBack provides spoken feedback and navigation assistance, and in Chrome, users can customize their browsing experience with extensions like high-contrast mode and screen magnifiers.

We're not all in tech making tech. But we can incorporate it into what we do.

By prioritizing accessibility, you will be part of creating a more inclusive digital world for everyone. Obviously, it must be done responsibly. You can't bankrupt the business creating custom one-off products for markets of two to three people who may or may not even want to buy it. After all, this book is about holistic growth—your spiritual growth in helping those who haven't been included creates process growth as you explore innovation and experimentation, which can drive efficiency growth as you strive to make great ideas viable and employee growth as team members find meaning in their work.

It's a powerful reminder that personalization and inclusivity go hand in hand when everyone can join the team as my mom did. When leaders embrace this philosophy, everyone wins and everyone grows.

I miss you, Mom.

And the thought of you wearing those basketball shoes still makes me smile.

Every One over Everyone

Your biggest opportunity might be the ultimate customization: building for, delivering to, and communicating with the unique human being before you, regardless of their abilities, culture, or gender.

Again, we're all snowflakes (and I use that positively). We're all unique beings. And while some of that uniqueness is driven by our abilities, cultural background, sexuality, and gender, much of it isn't. True growth occurs when we include every one. Not everyone. Every. One.

The best part? It's never been easier to do it.

L'Oréal's Skin Genius app uses AI to offer customized skincare recommendations for a more personalized skincare routine for every possible type and shade of skin, including my aging part Italian, part Quebecois, part Anglo skin. It measures fine lines, eye wrinkles, other wrinkles, firmness, pores, pigmentation, and radiance. I want radiant skin!

Sonic Drive-In embraced the spirit of individual expression by offering over 1.5 million drink combinations, allowing customers to become the architects of their own beverage creations. Coke did it, too. Their Freestyle machines let consumers design their ideal beverage. The good part for Coca-Cola? They gather the data on customers' preferences in the process. Nike's By You platform—it's literally called *by you*—allows customers to design their own sneakers, choosing from a variety of colors, materials, and patterns. Levi's Tailor Shop offers personalized denim fittings and alterations, so each pair of jeans fits perfectly and reflects the unique style of the person wearing them. Tesla has completely revolutionized not only the car itself but also the car-buying experience by allowing customers to customize their vehicles, choosing from a range of options and upgrades. IKEA's modular furniture systems allow customers to mix and match components, creating pieces that fit their specific spaces.

It's no longer enough to just offer a one-size-fits-all product or service.

A purpose-led personalized experience is an amazing experience.

And amazing experiences lead to growth.

THE FRICTIONLESS EXPERIENCE

Remove friction, and you're already halfway to success.

EXPERIENCES ARE like referees and umpires. You barely notice the excellent ones because everything just works. No hiccups, no barriers, and a series of seamless transitions between apps, online, and in person, all reinforcing that the company really gets you.

Part of personalized experience is understanding the whole human being and all the frustrations they exhibit along the way. Everyone has problems. And the biggest friction comes when a business isn't aware of the real problems people face.

Sometimes, they face emotional problems.
Sometimes, they face logistical problems.
Sometimes, they face financial problems.

Friction arises when you fail to solve the specific problem at a specific time in the journey. And friction is the enemy of a great experience. Remove it, and you're already halfway to success.

Seek and Solve

There's a tweet out there in the ether that's been reposted a bunch. To be honest, I don't even know if it's a real story. It could be a complete work of fiction and it wouldn't make me like it any less:

> the first thing our new hire did was fix a bug that's been bugging him forever as a user prior to joining. he then breathed a sigh of relief and submitted his two weeks' notice. wtf??

Can't you just picture that guy angrily going deep into the lines of code, finding the problem, deleting one character, and closing the laptop before walking out of the industrial park office for good? I can. I know about 20 of those people.

How many of you have faced friction during a company or product experience and contemplated this exact move? I have. I do. Daily.

Removing friction from a customer experience isn't just about making things easier. It's about actively seeking out the problems your customers face and working tirelessly to solve them. Shep Hyken, author of *The Convenience Revolution*, put it best: "Great companies don't just meet customer expectations—they exceed them by anticipating needs and addressing them before they become issues."

Bingo. Perfectly said, Shep.

The best customer experiences are those where the customer doesn't even realize there was friction at all because it was removed before it became a problem. We've all personally experienced this with Amazon. Their relentless focus on eliminating friction may be the case study to end all case studies. They're not an e-commerce company. They're a convenience company. One-click purchasing. Same-day delivery. Easy returns. They've made it so easy for customers to buy that we don't even think about the process.

Amazon seeks out potential pain points—whether it's a cumbersome checkout process or long delivery times—and solves them, often before the customer even realizes they exist.

One-click purchasing may be the smoothest, no-barriers-to-purchase move in all of e-commerce history.

Removing friction is an important step in creating amazing experiences that reinforce your purpose.

Easy is enjoyable.
Enjoyable is repeatable.
Repeatable is growth.

The Problem Isn't the Problem

When you think about the problems your customers or clients are facing, it's natural to focus on the most logical, obvious challenges. You sell a product, so they obviously have a product problem.

Or you sell a cheap product,
so clearly they have a money problem.

Or you sell an expensive product,
so clearly they have a too-much-money problem.

The reality is that they have a whole host of problems—most of which you'll never know. Those problems are rational, emotional, logical, and nonsensical. The more you know, the more you solve, but I'm willing to bet in many cases, the problem you think they have isn't the only problem you can solve.

I had a unique opportunity about a year ago to speak to a global pharmaceutical company that specializes in oncology. The entire Canadian team from across the country was in one hotel ballroom to reconnect and refocus on the year ahead.

I'm usually in the opening or closing keynote slot for events like this, but that doesn't mean that I'm always the actual opening or the actual closing. I've seen large gatherings like this open in a variety of different ways—but none more powerful than this one.

Before I went on, the team got to see two people whose lives had been saved by the medication this company makes and the mother of a young boy whose life had been saved thanks to the efforts of the people in the room. Those three people joined a moderated discussion on a virtual video call for all to experience.

You can only imagine how moving it was. One man had been literally given three months to live. He finally got access to the medication and lived to talk about it. Do you wanna inspire your people and reinforce the purpose that binds them? I can't think of a better way to do it.

Both of my parents died from cancer, so you can bet I was tearing up and trying to compose myself, so I wouldn't be a blubbering mess by the time I hit the stage. I wasn't sad for my parents or for my family. I was happy for these people and their loved ones who weren't forced to prematurely say goodbye.

Near the end of discussion, the moderator asked what I thought was a rather innocent question and I expected it would get a fairly straightforward answer.

"What could we do better?"

What could you do better? What could you do better than saving my life?

And these people had one problem, a health problem. The only friction was the life-or-death situation they found themselves in, and the only solution to that friction was the medication. They got the medication. Problem solved. Who's next?

But the mother of the young boy spoke up. She admitted that yes, all they needed was the medication, and once they got the medication, they thought that's all that they would need. But she continued, "This was my first time through this. As a mother, I didn't know what the rest of the experience was going to be. I desperately wanted to do the right thing for my son. You have thousands and thousands of patients and thousands and thousands of stories of what people have gone through—the highs and lows of getting better. But I didn't hear about any of it. What I really needed, what I most needed once I had the medication, was someone to hold my hand."

After the immediate health crisis was addressed, she was left with a massive emotional burden, feeling isolated and unsupported in a journey that didn't end with the administration of a drug.

She didn't just have a medical problem or a life-and-death problem or a medication problem. She had a parenting problem. She had a confidence problem. She had an emotional problem. She had an I-don't-know-what's-coming-next-and-I-don't-know-how-to-prepare problem.

She's not alone, either. In my experience, most organizations think the only problems their customers face are the problems specifically tied to the products they sell.

A bank might think their customers
only have a money problem.

A gym might think their members
only have a weight problem.

A car dealership might think their customers
only have a transportation problem.

A tech company might think their users
only have a software problem.

A restaurant might think their patrons
only have a hunger problem.

A retail store might think their shoppers
only have a product availability problem.

A healthcare provider might think their patients
only have a health problem.

But here's the truth: Customers don't just have product problems. They have emotional problems, logistical problems, confidence problems, and problems that touch on who they are as people and the complex relationships that shape their lives.

My good friend Kristi Herold is the founder and CEO of an organization called JAM, an adult sports and event company that has recreational leagues for softball, soccer, ultimate frisbee, and a ton of other sports. They own leagues all over North America and have grown tremendously since Kristi started it after we finished university over 30 years ago. Most participants in JAM are young adults who have the time to commit to a team or sport at least one night a week and who want to fill some of their downtime with sports that are fun and enjoyable. They're bored. They have time. And they want to be active with their friends.

Participants in JAM wouldn't typically say they were joining to date. Of course not. They are there to play sports. And aside from one cheeky tagline back in the early '00s—"Play the field"—Kristi and her team have never actively marketed JAM as a dating organization.

But over its history, thousands of babies have been born thanks to so many players meeting their love match on the playing field. Turns out people didn't just have a boredom problem. They had an I-want-to-meet-someone-but-I-don't-want-to-go-on-dating-apps problem.

As Kristi said, "Whether you're scoring a goal, cheering on your teammates, or just grabbing a drink after the game, you're connecting on a deeper level than a profile picture can provide."

The pharma people had solved the most obvious problem, but they missed an opportunity to address the deeper, more personal challenges that followed. That's an opportunity for purpose-focused growth.

A tech company that realizes users don't just have a software problem but also a fear of losing data and concerns about privacy can create solutions that go beyond the functionality of their apps.

A restaurant that understands its customers aren't just hungry but are also craving a sense of belonging or nostalgia can create a dining experience that resonates on a deeper emotional level.

A retail store that perceives its shoppers' underlying anxiety about finding the right fit, not just having the product in stock, can tailor the shopping experience to ease those worries.

A healthcare provider that sees beyond a patient's health issue and addresses their concerns about the affordability and accessibility of care can build stronger, more trusting relationships.

Use your purpose to focus and prioritize. Use your actions to solve the problems and create amazing experiences. Celebrate the growth that follows.

Use your purpose to focus and prioritize.

Join the Wolf PAC

While the hyperinflation and high-interest-rate environment that started in March 2022 caused a bunch of businesses to either slow down or tank completely, some businesses actually did better. Weird, huh?

Not really.

When there's a significant outside force like hyperinflation, a geopolitical crisis, a pandemic, or an environmental disaster, we typically see a change in consumer attitudes and behaviors. What used to be seamless can immediately become friction-filled as their needs change.

High prices that used to stroke egos and provide luxurious satisfaction can immediately become a major area of friction when the world enters an economic recession.

Problems can be, well, problems.
But they can also be catalysts to growth.

The organizations that spot the changes, identify the friction, and change their organization to respond can create a competitive difference and growth at the expense of others in the category.

This is the essence of what I call the problem as catalyst (PAC) framework; with it, you can turn life's frictions into competitive advantages.

PAC isn't about fixing minor issues within a customer journey. It's about responding to seismic shifts that create new problems for society. And when you use it, you are creating a competitive edge that propels you and your organization forward.

Here's the PAC framework.

1. A Spark Ignites Change to the Ecosystem

Every industry operates within an ecosystem, an interconnected network of businesses, customers, suppliers, and regulators that work in harmony... until something disrupts it.

The spark can come from anywhere—a technological breakthrough, a shift in consumer behavior, a regulatory change, or even a global crisis. The ecosystem that once hummed along smoothly is suddenly jolted by an outside force, creating new dynamics and challenges.

Example: The rise of social media was one such jolt. Before social platforms like Facebook, Threads, and Instagram became mainstream, brands were set in their ways, focusing on traditional advertising channels. The advent of social media fundamentally altered how consumers consumed content, interacted with each other, and engaged with brands. The old ecosystem, focused on traditional ads and content, was completely upended.

2. New Problems Emerge

The disruption creates ripple effects and creates new problems in its wake that didn't exist before the change. These issues can affect consumers, businesses, or both, creating vulnerabilities that need to be addressed quickly. If left unchecked, the problems can lead to a loss of market share, grumpy customers, and revenues that are described as "downhill."

Example: With the rise of social media and engaged consumers, a new problem emerged for brands: Consumers could now communicate with them in real time, publicly sharing their praise or criticism. This was a radical shift from the one-way communication channels that brands were used to. Suddenly, companies had to manage their reputations in a highly visible and fast-paced environment, where a single tweet could go viral and damage their brand in minutes.

3. Companies Rush to Solve the Problem and Innovate

When a new problem arises, companies scramble to find a solution. Some problems can be resolved with quick fixes, while others require a complete overhaul of existing business models. Regardless of the complexity, the opportunity to solve a pressing problem fuels innovation and drives companies to act.

Example: As brands grappled with the challenges of real-time communication on social media, they had to decide who would take ownership of this new responsibility. Marketing departments, customer service teams, PR firms, and IT departments all had stakes in the game, but none were fully equipped to handle the entire scope of social media management. The rush to solve this problem led to the next stage in the PAC framework.

4. Internal Problems Follow

Addressing a new problem often creates internal friction. Companies may add new services, processes, or responsibilities to existing roles, stretching budgets, complicating workflows, and requiring new training. This can lead to confusion, inefficiency, and a lack of accountability if not managed properly.

They want to do the right thing to solve the emerging problem, but that can create internal problems.

Example: As social media became a critical aspect of brand management, companies realized they lacked the internal expertise to handle it effectively. Customer service teams could answer inquiries, but they couldn't create engaging content. Marketing could craft campaigns, but they couldn't respond to technical issues. PR could manage crises, but they didn't have the tools to monitor social media in real time. This led to a fragmented approach that was neither efficient nor effective.

5. Adaptation Leads to Expertise and Competitive Advantage

To truly solve the problem and turn it into a competitive advantage, companies must develop new roles, behaviors, or even entire departments. By dedicating resources to these new areas, they can build expertise, streamline processes, and create a solution that not only addresses the initial problem but also sets them apart from the competition.

Example: The need for a comprehensive approach to social media management led to the creation of the community manager role. This new position was designed to be a hybrid, combining the skills of customer service, marketing, PR, and IT. Community managers became experts in social media, capable of engaging with customers, creating content, managing crises, and analyzing data—all in real time. The role didn't just solve the problem. It created a new competitive advantage for brands that could respond faster, engage more effectively, and build stronger relationships with their customers.

As another example, when COVID shut down eating in restaurants, some went down, some survived, and some thrived. Those that thrived used the problem before them as a catalyst to create an amazing experience and a competitive difference.

1 **A change happens to the ecosystem:** The pandemic shuts down the world.

2 **A new problem emerges:** Restaurants can't operate.

3 **Companies rush to solve the problem:** Food delivery apps offered tech, promotion, delivery, and payment for takeout.

4 **Internal problems follow:** Waitstaff were redundant, and new roles were needed to perfect the new process.

5. **New behaviors lead to expertise:** An internal skills transfer prioritized new logistics, new packaging, and new approaches to food quality.

As Seth Godin said,

> **Problems don't really care whether we acknowledge them or not. They still exist. What matters is how we choose to direct our energy, because our tomorrow is the direct result of the way we spend our resources today. Pick your problems, pick your future.**

Every problem is a catalyst. Will you let it define you or destroy you?

THE EMPLOYEE EXPERIENCE

Customers shouldn't read your purpose. They should experience it.

A TRULY EXCEPTIONAL customer experience begins with an empowered and inspired workforce.

When employees feel valued, understood, and motivated, *and* they understand the purpose of the organization and their role in bringing it to life, they create incredible experiences that customers remember, share, and cherish. They create great products. They design intuitive websites. They personalize and customize communications with specific audiences in mind. They create moments of magic, invest in personal growth, encourage team evolution, and drive organizational growth without even knowing how they're doing it.

All this dedication and passion doesn't happen by accident. It's cultivated in an environment where employees feel safe to express their ideas, connected to a purpose that matters, and supported by leaders who trust them to make decisions. When people understand what you believe in, they go beyond showing up. They bring their best selves to the table and are ready to go the extra mile.

Not because they have to. Because they want to.

Look, customers shouldn't read your purpose. They should experience it. And when they do, you're setting the stage for sustainable, meaningful growth. But they only experience it through the actions and decisions of your people.

So if you depend on people to deliver an amazing experience, you might want to ensure they have a pretty good experience themselves. Whether it's a frontliner with direct customer contact or a back-room analyst who doesn't even interact with the plants, positive experiences are contagious.

For one assignment, we were collaborating with our friends from Livewire, an agency that communicates change inside organizations and who believes that "change is only successful when employees feel it's happening with them, not to them." Together, we identified something that exists in most organizations.

It's the gap that exists between where you would like your CX to be and where your EX is. We call it the CX-EX gap. The gap exists because the quality of your customer experience is directly tied to the quality of your employee experience. Your employees are the ones who deliver the service, interact with customers, and bring your brand's promise to life. If they're disengaged, undervalued, or frustrated, it's impossible for them to create the exceptional experiences you're striving for.

On the other hand, employees who feel heard, seen, and appreciated are far more likely to go above and beyond, creating memorable customer interactions and incredible experiences and helping to drive growth. That's a good thing.

There are only two ways to close the CX-EX gap: improve your employee experience, or lower your standards for customer experience. Lowering your standards is not a viable option in a market where customers expect more than ever before. That would be a race to the bottom, and it's one that no business can afford to win.

Improving employee experience, on the other hand, is a win-win. An exceptional employee experience isn't the sole responsibility of senior management; it's a collective effort. Employees need to feel valued, heard, and understood. They need to see that their work contributes to something meaningful and that they have a valuable role to play in bringing the company's purpose to life. When employees are empowered and engaged, they are more likely to treat customers as unique individuals, solving their problems with empathy and care.

In an era when experiences are top of the list of what people are seeking, organizations cannot afford to ignore the EX side of the equation. Great customer experiences don't happen in a vacuum; they are the result of a thriving, motivated, and engaged workforce.

Lattes and Leadership

I really like Boston. It's a wonderful city with a great vibe, and some of my favorite people in the speaking world live there like Tom Webster, Tamsen Webster, Ann Handley, Laura Gassner Otting, Jay Acunzo, and others. If it wasn't for the Bruins and Red Sox, it might be a perfect city. Given the proximity to my home and the great venues, I love speaking there, too.

Recently, I was doing a keynote there at the Lenox Hotel for a large US retailer. The Lenox is a wonderfully charming hotel. Interestingly, my talk was about CX and I ended up having an amazing experience myself minutes before I went onstage.

It started off as a regular morning. After a call with our team from my room, I went down to the hotel restaurant to enjoy a quick (and light) breakfast and my usual morning latte. If nothing else, I'm a creature of habit.

I ordered and waited, enjoying some time to review my notes. A few minutes passed, and then Haley, a member of the restaurant staff, approached my table.

"Are you the one waiting on a latte?" she asked.

"Yup, that's me."

Haley informed me that the espresso machine had just gone down. "I tried to fix it, but no luck," she said, clearly frustrated by the situation. Of course, I was going to say "No biggie," order a regular coffee, and be on my way.

But before I could even respond, she continued, "I'm going to Starbucks. What would you like?"

I was taken aback by her offer. "Oh, it's okay. You don't have to do that," I said, not wanting to trouble her.

But Haley wouldn't hear of it. "It's no problem at all," she insisted. "I'm going anyway. I want some chai." And off she went.

A short while later, Haley returned with a Starbucks latte in hand. But that wasn't the end of it. She refused to charge me for the drink. This simple act of kindness was more than just good customer experience. It was a perfect example of what happens when an employee truly understands the purpose of their organization and knows how to reinforce it.

Most positive CX is proactive. Solving problems before they become problems. But sometimes, great CX happens in the moments when you have to be reactive as opposed to proactive. For the proactive stuff, you need to invest in research, infrastructure, technology, design, and more to remove friction. But that reactive stuff? That usually depends on your staff being able, being knowledgeable, being empowered, and being willing to do it.

If they don't want to do it,
it doesn't matter how much training they have.

If they don't want to do it,
it doesn't matter how prepared they are.

If they don't want to do it,
it doesn't matter how much budget they have.

If they don't want to do it,
it doesn't matter how empowered they are.

And in my experience, they want to deliver great CX when they receive great EX.

Haley didn't have access to fancy technology or an elaborate system to solve the problem. Instead, she relied on her understanding of what the Lenox Hotel stands for—creating exceptional experiences for its guests, no matter what. She saw an obstacle and turned it into an opportunity to go above and beyond. She knew what the expectations were, she knew what she could do to deliver on them, and she knew she had the support of her leaders to make the decision in the moment. During moments like this, the human touch—driven by a clear understanding of purpose—makes all the difference.

One part of an outstanding employee experience is what Haley demonstrated. She was the one on the front line. She was the one who was going to get grief and have

If they don't want to do it, it doesn't matter how much training they have.

to deal with a grumpy guest. If she has to deal with it, shouldn't she be the one to decide how she handles it?

When frontline employees lack the authority to solve customer issues they understand best and can resolve the fastest and still have to face the resulting customer anger—from a decision they didn't even make—there's a technical term for it: "a crappy employee experience."

Haley's initiative at the Lenox Hotel showcased the power of empowering frontline employees. If only Major League Baseball did the same.

Sorry, It's Not My Call

In 2014, Major League Baseball introduced the expanded use of video replay review to help get calls on the field right. It was a big step forward for the game.

It allows managers to challenge certain plays they feel were called incorrectly. If they are right and the call is wrong, they retain their ability to challenge. If they are wrong and the umpire's call is right, they lose it.

It's not a perfect system, but it generally ensures greater accuracy and penalizes anyone who wants to use the review delay to their advantage. In 2023, there were over 1,400 replay reviews, with nearly half of those resulting in overturned calls. That's pretty good.

But there's one metric no one has bothered to measure: the mental health of the umpires who are being openly challenged and proven right or wrong in front of thousands of people. If you consider them employees (which they are), the entire process has created a horrible employee experience. See, the umpires aren't the ones who get to review the footage and revise their own calls.

Someone else does that. From head office. In New York. From the comfort of their office while the umpires are left to announce their decision *and* face the boos or cheers that it generates.

Yup. Umpires are now often blamed for decisions made in New York by someone they've never even met.

Irate managers and players know full well that the umpires have no control over these decisions, yet they direct their frustration and anger at the only visible authority figure.

Sound familiar?

This scenario couldn't be more stereotypically corporate: a faceless, nameless decision-maker at headquarters in New York using tools the frontline staff don't have access to, making an unchallengeable final decision that significantly affects the experience on the ground, and it's the frontline employee who has to deliver the news and face the consequences of someone else's actions. The customer knows the waitstaff haven't implemented the policy they're enforcing, but that doesn't stop the customer from directing their frustration at them anyhow.

This speaks volumes about how frustrated humans treat frontline workers and the difficult position we put those employees in when we don't give them the tools to defuse the situation or the authority to make the call themselves. Leadership is about more than making the right decisions; it's about empowering your people to make decisions and giving them the resources they need to manage customer interactions effectively.

With overall life frustrations on the rise, the combination of perceived consumer injustice and inflexible corporate policy, often delivered with scripted dialogue, has led to a surge in the mistreatment of frontline employees.

Real leadership involves making decisions *and* supporting those on the front lines who have to deal with the consequences of those decisions.

Tell Me What You Want, What You Really Want

Often, we think employees crave perks like competitive salaries, career advancement opportunities, and a dental plan. Sure, those things are nice (and important), but they're not the whole story. These are some of the things that people really want.

Meaning over Money

Employees want meaning. They want to know that their work contributes to something bigger—whether that's solving a customer's problem, achieving a company goal, or simply making someone's day a little better.

Flexibility over Fixed

Today's employees also want flexibility. Is that any surprise from the generation who feels tied down owning music? The ability to work from anywhere—whether it's from home or on a beach in Bali—has gone from a perk to an expectation.

Recognition over Routine

Recognition matters. And not the generic "good job" kind, but sincere, specific praise that makes employees feel valued. This can happen informally in the moment and formally on the calendar.

Development over Dormancy

With one eye on their job and another on their career, employees want opportunities to grow, develop, and take on new challenges. Learning while doing brings energy to the short term and benefits to the long term.

Connection over Isolation

Finally, employees want connection. They want to feel part of something bigger, like a company mission or a team. Meaningful connections—whether with colleagues, mentors, or the company's mission—can transform an employee's experience.

It's simple: They want work to be a place where they find meaning, flexibility, recognition, growth, and connection. And if you can provide that, you'll have a team that's not merely satisfied but truly inspired.

THE RUNNER
SAVANNAH BANANAS

DEFINED BY ACTIONS

While he could have applied his purpose to any one of hundreds of areas of the business, Jesse Cole was driven by the need to save the team, not to mention his own life.

Jesse and his wife, Emily, were heavily in debt and had to sell their house, max out their credit cards, and take out personal loans to keep the team afloat. And this wasn't Silicon Valley. Venture capitalists weren't exactly lining up for a seed round for a team in the lowest rung of collegiate baseball in the country. And the initial sales drive? It resulted in one new ticket sale. They couldn't afford to throw money at the problem. It had to be focused. They needed to act on purpose. It wasn't the slogan or even the name that would define their success. It would be their actions.

So they took the Brand Belief under their arms and prioritized fixing the experience.

If the Savannah Bananas had an Essential Do, I think this is what it would be:

> **We believe there's a better way to do almost everything *so* we challenge the way things are supposed to be and make them better than we ever thought they could be.**

Improving the baseball experience is where Jesse Cole and the Bananas really showed how relentlessly they would help the team thrive. As Jesse said in a keynote speech,

> **The best business model in the world is to stop doing what your customers hate. It's that simple. Do what they love. If you want to be fans-first, you have to look at everything.**

And look at everything he did.

Fans thought it was boring.
So Jesse created nonstop entertainment from the start of the game to the end. They turned up the music and got people dancing.

Fans hated extra ticket fees.
The Bananas built their own ticketing system so they could eliminate all ticket fees and convenience fees. It also allowed them to pay the taxes on the tickets instead of charging the fans for it. They also refused

$1 million from resellers, which would line their pockets with money but cost the fans more.

Fans hated the price of the food.
The Bananas now controlled all the concessions and included food in the price of the ticket.

Fans hated all the ads in the ballpark.
The Bananas eliminated advertising.

Fans didn't think the Bananas were connected to the community.
Each game featured a community nonprofit.

When describing his approach to improvement, Jesse called out the problem with waiting in line.

> **The metrics that our operations focus on solely is time-in-line. Time-in-line is everything... You're not doing anything. It's a friction point. It's a frustration point. And so, we time every night. We know that if we're over five minutes, we're detracting from the experience.**

But all of those changes still weren't enough. Remember, Jesse is described as someone willing to reject industry norms. Jesse looked at that statement and said, "Hold my beer."

See, Jesse found that the biggest friction in the fan experience was one he had no control over. The biggest barriers to an amazing experience were the rules of baseball—the very things that governed the way the sport was played by every team. It's not like teams can go rogue and radically rewrite the established rules for their own ballpark.

Oh yes, they can.

Jesse rejected industry norms, turned his back on the establishment, and left the league so he could really change the experience. Jesse invented Banana Ball—a new way to play baseball that created a new way to enjoy baseball.

Banana Ball's rule changes are designed to speed up the game and increase excitement.

Games are limited to two hours.

Each inning is a game within a game: The team that scores the most runs in an inning earns a point. The team with the most points at the end of the game wins.

There's no bunting.

Players can't step out of the batter's box.

Coaches can't visit the mound.

And my personal favorite rule: If a batter hits a foul ball and a fan catches it, the batter is out.

That's Banana Ball. An entirely new product. With entirely new rules. Against entirely new competitors. (They had to build their own teams to play against.) For an entirely new experience. For the fans. And for his employees.

The Savannah Bananas didn't just focus on the fans. They made sure their employees and players were aware of the purpose, understood their role in bringing it to life, and had as much fun as the fans in the process.

They created a winning culture where everyone felt like they were part of something special with an employee experience that was completely different than on a normal baseball team.

As Jesse likes to say, "Love your customers more than you love your products. Love your employees more than you love your customers."

The Bananas don't recruit players based solely on traditional baseball skills—those skills are for other teams in other leagues with different rules and different beliefs. The Bananas prioritize personality, showmanship, and a willingness to entertain. They ask for a video cover letter so they can see their personality in action. They ask for a fans-first essay on how they get the Bananas' core beliefs, and then finally, applicants have to submit a future résumé, because "we're not interested what you did in the past, we want to know what you want to do in the future."

During tryouts, they have a TikTok station, a dancing station, an interview-that-follows-a-wrestling-match station, and more.

Players are encouraged to express themselves, engage with fans, and participate in choreographed dances and on-field skits. They're also encouraged to engage with fans and be a part of the entertainment, not just the game. And that results in a meaningful purpose that goes well beyond winning or losing.

The New York Yankees prohibit players, coaches, and executives from having any facial hair beyond a mustache. The Savannah Bananas are encouraged to "express themselves." If you want your players to create an experience, you have to create one for them where they can be themselves.

But you can't expect players and staff to automatically know *what to do* even though they may be brilliant at what they do. I would say that the Bananas do a great job training their people, but Jesse has said, "I don't like the word 'training.' Dogs are trained. Humans should be coached, mentored, and educated."

I'll repeat that for those at the back:

> **Dogs are trained. Humans should be coached, mentored, and educated.**

So, they developed Fans First U where the Bananas spend days onboarding staff and players. Before anyone puts on a uniform, they first hear stories about the art of being fans-first.

Overall, the Bananas foster (mmmmmm . . .) a culture of creativity, fun, and empowerment where everyone is encouraged to challenge the status quo and contribute to the team's success. The organization prioritizes work-life balance, offering flexible schedules and promoting a positive and inclusive work environment.

The Bananas prove that when you cultivate a culture of fun and empowerment where people are coached, mentored, and educated, your employees won't just swing for the fences, they'll dance their way around the bases as they head for home.

7

"A leader should never stifle debate.

But if you have to, just say

'It is what it is' and then stare at

your iPhone until they leave."

HENRY FORD

ADOPTED THROUGH COMMUNICATIONS

(THE SAY PART)

Great leaders aren't just remembered; they're quoted.

Who Said What

Within our agency, one of my business partners, Robin Whalen, and I often debate who's funnier. On one hand, I was a professional comedian for 20 years. On the other hand, Robin's funnier.

Among the many strengths that Robin brings to the table is her incredible ability to channel the wisdom of those who mentored her throughout her career. Not a day goes by without her saying, "You know, my old boss at Vickers & Benson used to say..." There's usually a backstory, a wild time filled with things we would never dream of doing these days, and a lesson. She seamlessly weaves in a piece of wisdom—verbatim—from her bosses that she not only remembers but uses.

While she always speaks highly of those leaders and is genuinely proud of the time she spent with them, what really sticks with her—and, by extension, with the rest of us—are the lines she quotes. And I think most of us are like that.

Great leaders aren't just remembered; they're quoted.

This is why I'm so opposed to people—speakers, authors, thought leaders—quoting themselves. This pet peeve is something that Scott Stratten, Mitch Joel, and I share. People writing something in a predesigned template and miraculously attributing it to themselves.

That's not how respect works. You can't impose it. You have to earn it.

And earning it means *other* people quote you. You don't get to judge whether your words are brilliant enough to be quoted. The very idea of a quote is that someone else is referencing your words. Besides, let's be honest, most of the quotes that people share from themselves aren't exactly worthy of being repeated, let alone quoted. As Scott has said, "Words aren't quotes."

Great leaders aren't just remembered; they're quoted.

Think about all the great leaders we talk about in business, the arts, politics, and sports. Usually, we associate them with specific quotes, lines, statements, and ideas that have stood the test of time. There's a reason for that. Great leaders have the ability to capture the essence of what they fundamentally believe, what others can do to help, why they want to join along, and what the future will look like if everyone works together—all in a few memorable lines.

Martin Luther King Jr. said, "I have a dream that my four little children will one day live in a nation where they will not be judged by the color of their skin but by the content of their character."

This line has echoed through generations because it encapsulates a powerful vision of equality and justice in a few brief words. Heck, the entire speech is often referred to as the "I have a dream" speech even though it wasn't officially called anything. That's how memorable his line was.

Great leaders are quoted because they (or their speechwriters) took the time to put as much care into communicating their thoughts as they did into formulating them.

Words Are Worth Fighting For

Dan Wieden may not be an instantly recognizable name to everyone outside advertising, but for those of us in the space, he's nothing short of a legend.

Sadly, Dan passed away in 2022, but his legacy is one that continues to influence business. He was cofounder of a great agency, Wieden+Kennedy, which has been behind some of the most iconic campaigns in history.

But Dan? I think Dan delivered the most efficient ROI in the history of capitalism. Dan wrote three words. And those three words not only changed the trajectory of one client and one category, I think Dan's three words fundamentally changed the world.

Dan wrote "Just do it."

The story behind those three simple words is as compelling as the tagline itself. Dan drew inspiration from an unlikely source. It wasn't an issue of *Communication Arts*, a Maya Angelou quote, or a long-lost script from a forgotten film.

It was an inmate on death row.

The prisoner, Gary Gilmore, facing execution, was asked if he had any last words. His reply? "Let's do it." Obviously, Dan found something profound in those words. Maybe they encapsulated a sense of resolve, a readiness to face whatever comes next, no matter how daunting. Dan tweaked the phrase, changing "Let's" to "Just," and with that, "Just do it" was born.

Dan thought that those three words precisely communicated what Nike believed and what they hoped to inspire people to do. He believed that "Just do it" was more than a tagline. It was a distillation of Nike's core belief: to bring inspiration and innovation to every athlete in the world.

When Dan first presented the tagline to his team, it was met with skepticism... and he was the boss! His team thought it was too simple and lacked substance.

But Dan fought for it. Dan fought for three words.

He convinced his team, and they took it to Phil Knight, Nike's cofounder. Phil's initial reaction was like Dan's team's—he wasn't impressed. Dan didn't back down.

Again, he fought for three words.

He argued passionately that "Just do it" was the best way to encapsulate Nike's mission, to inspire not only athletes, but everyone, to strive for greatness. He understood that for a brand to truly resonate, it had to communicate its fundamental beliefs in a way that was both simple and powerful.

He knew that true growth wasn't going to come from inspiring elite athletes to be better. It would come from inspiring everyone else to be athletic.

As you know, Dan's persistence paid off. I could present data and charts and studies on Nike's growth. I'll save you the time and just say they've done very well.

Dan Wieden's genius was in both crafting the line *and* fighting for the line. All because he knew it would drive personal growth, which, in turn, would drive Nike's growth.

Dan didn't give up. He wasn't resigned to going back to the office and writing 10 more lines because the client didn't like his recommendation. He wasn't resigned to doing all the insightful strategy work only to give up when he was steps from the finish line.

He hadn't come this far to just come this far.

And neither have you.

Far too many leaders do all the thinking, create strategies and action plans, have clear priorities on how they're going to achieve growth, and they think that once the heavy lifting is done, well, the heavy lifting is done.

Nope. Now, you gotta sell it.

It's not enough to just send out an email.
It's not enough to just do a deck.
It's not enough to just print a poster.
It's not enough to just do a Teams call.
It's not enough to just write a LinkedIn post.
It's not enough to just do a campaign.
It's not enough to just ask everyone to
ensure that they "get it."

You need them to adopt your ideas and passions. You need them—all of them—to understand you, join you, and work on your behalf to drive the growth you planned for.

And all of that only happens if you put as much care and attention into communicating it as you did into planning it.

Great leaders don't just state a purpose; they inspire others to believe in it.

You have time. And if you don't, make it.
You have the permission. And if you don't, get it.
You have the resources. And if you don't, find them.
You have the skills. And if you don't, learn them.
You have their respect. And if you don't, earn it.

Put This on Repeat

Our parents used to tell us "I'm only going to say it once" or "Don't make me repeat myself." It was a classic move to get us to listen the first time. But in leadership? That mantra won't get you very far. In fact, if you want to be an effective leader, you have to actually do the opposite: You have to become the chief repeating officer.

Author Patrick Lencioni reminded us, "The cost of under-communicating is so much higher than the cost of over-communicating." In other words, if you repeat one too many times, you might get some eyeballs. If you repeat one too few times, you get less alignment, less inspiration, less focus, and less growth.

Until you've repeated a message seven or eight times, people won't believe it's true. They'll have doubts. They'll forget. They'll get distracted by the million other things going on in their workdays.

That's where the chief repeating officer role comes in.

Enough with stating the company's purpose once at the start of the AGM. You need to remind everyone—constantly—from the leadership team to the newest hire, what's truly important. You have to be a relentless advocate and cheerleader for the company's purpose and priorities by reiterating them at every opportunity.

Here's a fun test.

Ask your team to do an impression of you. Shoot it and show it to the entire company. Listen to what they say in their impression, and you'll get a pretty good idea what they hear from you most often.

My old agency, Havas, did a video of people doing impressions of me when I left, and apparently, the only thing I ever said was "Yeah, yeah, yeah." It was insightful *and* humbling.

Look, if you're doing it right, your people should be able to do a pretty good impression of you using your purpose as the script. They should know what you're going to say before you say it because they've heard it so many times.

It's not just about repetition, though. It's about consistency and clarity of message. The message has to be clear, and it has to stay the same, especially in times of uncertainty. The more you repeat it, the more it becomes ingrained in the company's culture.

To achieve growth, you keep everyone aligned and focused on what really matters. And they can't read your mind.

So don't just say it. Repeat it.

Don't Ask Them to Do, Ask Them to Be

I don't know Jonah Berger, but I've done a couple of gigs with him. I like and respect his work.

One of the things I love from Jonah's book *Magic Words* revolves around a simple but powerful concept: how to turn actions into identities. Whether we're trying to get your team onside or your customers inside, the subtle shift in language Jonah suggests can make a significant difference in the results we achieve.

As leaders, we often rely on verbs to encourage specific actions.

Do this. Do that. Don't do that. Do this instead.

Don't litter. Pick up your garbage. Read this book. Don't put that there.

On the surface, these instructions seem clear, logical, and direct. But Jonah's research reveals that a quick and minor adjustment can lead to a major increase in compliance.

Instead of telling people what to do, he suggests framing the action as part of their identity. Instead of asking people to help with a task, invite them to be a helper. Instead of asking people to vote, inspire them to be a voter.

Turn a verb into a noun.

In one study cited by Jonah, asking people to "be a helper" increased helping behavior by nearly a third. Asking people to "be a voter" instead of "to vote" boosted voter turnout by 15 percent.

That, my friends, is growth.

Just as we all love the sound of our own names, we also have a desire to see ourselves in a positive light. By framing an action as an identity, we make it easier for people to align their behavior with that identity.

This is huge thinking for anyone who wants to drive actions that connect to purpose and drive growth.

Instead of asking colleagues to lead,
encourage them to be leaders.
Instead of telling employees to collaborate,
invite them to be collaborators.

Change the words. Change the outcomes.
Encourage identity over instructions.

It's not only about what people should do but who they can be.

Be a leader. Transform intentions into actions. And actions into lasting change.

Say Less, Win More

In the early weeks of the pandemic, as the world grappled with the confusion, one message stood out amid the chaos: "Flatten the curve."

These words became the rallying cry for millions. They captured the essence of what needed to be done to prevent healthcare systems from being overwhelmed. "Flatten the curve" was repeated endlessly by public health officials and media outlets.

It was clear. It was directive. But more than anything, it was simple.

In a time of incredible uncertainty, the power of the phrase was in its simplicity. It took a ridiculously complex situation with viral transmission rates, healthcare capacity, and societal behavior and distilled it into a single, easy-to-understand goal.

"Flatten the curve" did more than inform; it unified.

People everywhere, regardless of their background or level of understanding, could grasp what was at stake and what their role was in addressing it. Kinda like what you need your team to do.

Enough of the MBA speak handcrafted by a bunch of senior execs who want to show off their private school education and justify their inflated salaries. You're not presenting to the UN. You're presenting to your team, and you don't just need them to respect you. You need them to understand you.

You think what you have to say is important? It is. But you're up against the other stuff competing for their attention. Without simplicity, your message will be just another pop-up, just another notification, just another email, just another presentation. And most importantly, just another corporate initiative to drive growth.

Do you realize how ridiculous internal comms have become?

This tweet from @gossipbabies captures the absurdity of modern internal communications:

> Working at any office is like "Ok we're transitioning to Salarya, but payroll is still in Bullfrog—did you see my Noosecock post? Submit your timecard on Fireplayce then jizz me on smackdog. Do NOT upload to Crackerz without Yammer approval."

This tweet, while hilarious, also highlights a significant problem: When communication becomes overly complex and jargon-laden, it's not just ineffective—it's downright counterproductive. People tune out. They miss the point. They get frustrated. They move on without joining in.

And it's not only about simplifying language; it extends to the very look and feel of how you present your ideas.

As Ben Schott, former branding and advertising columnist for *Bloomberg Opinion*, brilliantly articulated, many of the world's biggest companies have recently undergone a process that he calls "de-branding," where they strip back the complexity of their logos and visual identities.

He discovered that "Burger King lost weight. *Rolling Stone* found a cleaner edge. VW shed its depth and shadow, as did Kia, Pfizer, Amazon, Nissan, Durex, Intel, Toyota, and a host of other major brands."

This trend toward "design sobriety," where logos and visual identities are simplified, is driven by several forces, including the pressure of mobile-first design. When something has to be legible on tiny smartphone screens, the old adage "Can you make the logo bigger?" has become "Can you make the logo simpler?"

Simplicity—both visually and with language—cuts through the noise. It creates a direct line of communication and reduces the risk of misinterpretation.

I think one of the most persuasive videos in our history—one that drove more action tied to purpose than all but a few videos before it—may not be that obvious.

It was from 2015. Marine biologist Christine Figgener filmed her team removing a plastic straw from a sea turtle's nose.

That was it. A plastic straw was stuck in a sea turtle's nose, and when her team removed it, viewers could see the pain and anguish the turtle experienced.

The video was raw, emotional, and, most importantly, simple. It showed—in stark detail—the impact of plastic pollution on marine life. And you know what happened next. It helped create a global movement to ban plastic straws.

What made the video so powerful wasn't the shocking imagery alone; it was the simplicity of the message it conveyed: "This is what happens when we don't act." It didn't even need any words. And it didn't need elaborate explanations. The visual communicated the urgent need for change.

People will adopt your ideas and passions through your communication of them. This simple visual led to a tangible shift in consumer expectations and corporate behavior more effectively than (gulp) any ad created by an agency that came before it.

Simplicity works.

Metaphors can turn bland into brilliance.

Banish the Buzz, Master the Metaphor

If your team is going to adopt your purpose and drive growth, they have to:

a understand what your purpose is and

b know what they're supposed to do to reinforce it so growth is realized.

If only it was that easy.

Sadly, leaders often communicate with a desire to impress instead of a desire to be understood. Their charts, graphs, and data points get lost in translation, and the team feels more lost than found. Their buzzword bingo cards may be full, but their hearts are empty and their heads are noisy.

Bypass buzzwords, cut charts, delete data, and opt to use a metaphor instead. It'll improve comprehension and connection to purpose, drive the right behaviors, and help stimulate growth.

A powerful metaphor can make the complex simple by stripping down complicated ideas into relatable, digestible nuggets.

Want to explain market dominance? Instead of mind-numbing graphs and a virtual call with your CFO, try comparing it to a shark ruling the ocean. Suddenly, the concept becomes vivid, memorable, and—let's be honest—a tad more exciting.

Beyond clarity, metaphors can offer up a different perspective that opens the door to fresh, innovative ideas. You're not looking at market dominance; you're looking at the world through the shark's eyes, not yours. That's way more fun and much more engaging. You want to generate ideas on growth, and before you know it, everyone's playing the theme from *Jaws* and watching the Land Shark sketch from SNL's first season.

Metaphors have a knack for sticking in your brain. A clever comparison or witty wordplay is memorable because it acts as a mental anchor that keeps everyone aligned with the task before them. You could have people memorize everything about market dominance through the shark's eyes—having an overdeveloped sense of smell, prioritizing speed and agility, not being shy to ambush, etc. Or you could print a slogan on T-shirts that says "Never Stop Swimming." That one phrase is the only callback your people need to remind them of the entire metaphor.

Metaphors can turn bland into brilliance.
Complex into creative.
And sucky into sticky.
So, ditch the jargon and embrace the metaphor.

Go Home, McDonald's— You're Drunk

I think McDonald's means something different to each of us even though we've all grown up with it either directly or indirectly. Maybe you're a character person and love Ronald. Or maybe you're an efficiency aficionado and connect with the operational approach. Maybe you're more of a commuter, and to you, McDonald's is the drive-thru place you get your coffee before arriving three minutes late for a 9 a.m. IRL meeting. Heck, to you, McDonald's may represent the evil meat grinder who contradicts your vegetarian philosophy.

To me, McDonald's is couple of things. It's a reminder of a simpler time when my mom would take us *on the bus* to a McDonald's in Montreal because we had some money left over after buying essentials and we could afford the treat of a flat burger with a pickle on it. But it's also a huge treat for our family. Not because of financial pressures but because of what we think we should feed our children—we don't think McDonald's is evil, but we do think all foods that aren't optimally healthy should be consumed in moderation. And for the record, if you've seen me, you know that's a family philosophy, not a personal philosophy.

Regardless, what McDonald's *isn't* for me is a late-night go-to. I'm a night owl, but I'm not going to clubs or roaming the streets until the wee hours of the morning. I'm watching YouTube Shorts like other people my age. But for some, McDonald's is that place—when you're drunk or high and have been partying your integrity off and you need some food to satisfy your craving for fast food.

In the UK, McDonald's recognized that their late-night customers weren't the same as their daytime customers. Daytime crowds roll up to the cash, ponder their choices, and speak in complete and polite sentences. Late-night crowds burst through the doors or mumble incoherently to the drive-thru speaker. They're not interested in jingles or cheerful, all-ages messages.

I think McDonald's purpose is that when it comes to meals and snacks, everyone deserves the right to "love it"—even those who are inebriated in the middle of the night. So why not customize communication of the purpose for that audience?

Earlier, I spoke about the importance of personalization of a product or service. Well, that also extends to communications. If you want people to get onside, you have to speak to them in their own language—whether it's an actual language, an informal language, or words and phrases that they use. Trust me, your team does not use the same language to describe your process or your philosophy as you do.

You might make the decisions, but they drive the truth. How they describe something is usually a pretty good indication of how they feel about it or how they assess it.

You report to the board, "We're running a lean operation." Your team reports to clients, "We're understaffed."

You proudly announce, "We have an open-door policy." Your team whispers, "Communications suck."

You tell new hires, "We encourage a high-performance culture." Your people tell them, "The workload is unmanageable."

You embrace the approach of "thoughtful and deliberate decision-making." They say that really means "decisions take forever."

If you want them to adopt your ideas, you have to adopt their language.

Just like McDonald's brilliantly did with the drunk crowd.

McDonald's launched a campaign with the tagline "We speak late night": Ads playfully mimicked the slurred, jumbled speech of someone who might have had a few too many drinks. They included headlines like "A Mig Back Congo peas" (Big Mac combo, please) and "Ferret oh Frish extra tata" (Filet-O-Fish extra tartar) to cleverly capture the mood of the late-night drive-thru experience.

This was a masterclass in personalized communication. McDonald's didn't slap a late-night label on their usual content. They created an entirely different tone that aligned with a specific audience's mood and mindset. They spoke directly to those customers in their language at their moment of need.

That's precisely why our strategic approach to clients has to be so flexible. Instead of giving clients a glossary of what we mean when we say "creative platform" or "Brand Belief," we adopt *their* language so we can drive efficiency. When I'm briefed for a keynote speech, one of the first questions I ask is "What do you call the people in the room? Are they your partners, your clients, your franchisees, your network, what?" There's no feeling like saying something onstage and seeing the facial reactions of a few people in the crowd who are thinking, "He doesn't get us."

When you lose the room, it's really difficult to get it back. And incorrect language is one of the fastest ways to lose it.

Do You Believe?

In the spring of 1998, Cher recorded the song "Believe." At its core, "Believe" is a great song. It was seemingly written by a committee of people including Cher (although she didn't get a credit for writing), but I tend to enjoy the covers more than Cher's original. Have you heard Adam Lambert's version? Incredible.

While recording the track, producer Mark Taylor wasn't happy with the verse. He kept telling Cher to sing it better. She responded, "You know, you want someone to sing it better, get another singer." Then she walked out.

Taylor had started experimenting with a pitch machine (commonly known as Auto-Tune), and the next day, he applied it to the song—with the now-famous electronic-sounding results. That the song was a hit wasn't entirely because of Cher; it was partially because of the pitch machine.

We can argue about what sounds better in music, but I know what sounds better in leadership.

Far too many people rely on things akin to Auto-Tune to deliver their messages instead of finding the skill to deliver it in a compelling way on their own. They worry about the imperfections of delivery, so they script their remarks to be perfect. They use a pitch machine to pitch their people. And their people can hear it a mile away.

I spent enough time writing about authenticity in *Think Do Say* that I'm not going to completely revisit it here. So consider this a reminder. Authenticity is being comfortable with your imperfections. And if you let others speak on your behalf, you're losing your imperfections, decreasing trust, and lessening the likelihood that other people will adopt your authentic ideas. I'm very active on LinkedIn, and sometimes, people ask me if I write my own LinkedIn posts or if I have someone who helps me. While there are different people who post on behalf of Church+State, I write every word of every post from my personal account. No one else even has access. Every like, comment, message, or share comes directly from me.

I want to control it. I want it to be my voice. And I know how frustrated I get when I receive LinkedIn messages that I know were written by "the company who helps with leads," not the individual messaging me.

It takes longer, it's tougher to craft, and I wouldn't have it any other way.

"But you can't scale that!" skeptics will say. In my experience, the people who scale using others charge a lower fee for more gigs. Whenever I get a pitch from one of those "We'll deliver leads" companies, I always reply, "Our projects start at $100K. Show me one instance where you have delivered a project of that size to an agency of our size."

They never write back. Because scale to them means quantity, not quality.

Maintain your quality of communications and you can maintain your quality of leads.

Admittedly, I do have a very specific approach. I'm not on LinkedIn 24 hours a day. My colleagues would hate me if I was. I do all my reading and most of my writing on the weekend. I write posts immediately after reading an article, and I schedule the distribution of posts throughout the week. I also write stuff randomly during the week when I think of it, and unless it's time sensitive, I just throw it into Buffer and it comes out when it comes out.

For me, LinkedIn works best as my "open mic night." I'm passionate about what I believe in, but my posts are usually the start of a thought or an immediate gut reaction to an article. Sometimes, I totally change my mind because of comments. Sometimes, I learn more. And sometimes, I double down and fight for what I think is right. And even then, I can certainly be wrong.

I hope I'm respectful and supportive.

I know some of you disagree
(because you've told me so),
but know that that is my intention.

It's open mic night! Sometimes it'll suck. Sometimes it won't.

But it's always about starting something as opposed to finishing something...

People buy your imperfections; they don't buy your machine.

So, ditch the script, tune out the Auto-Tune, and keep your own pitch in your pitch.

From Words to Wins: The Brand Narrative Blueprint

In the world of branding (and rebranding), we often hear terms like "strategy," "naming," "palettes," "fonts," "logos," and "design" thrown around. And while these are crucial elements of any branding effort, there's one component that often gets overlooked but is absolutely vital: the brand narrative.

We created our version of the brand narrative when a client in Houston asked us to rebrand the organization. We do a ton of brands in Canada and the US, and our team has strategists, creatives, and designers to do the work.

If you want to
drive growth,
you still need a
singular, unifying
narrative to do it.

This particular client said, "I want you to rebrand my company, but I don't want you to change the logo and I don't want you to change colors and I don't want to change the fonts and we don't need new signage on the building so don't bother with that. What we need is a new story to tell. We have all the pieces to drive incredible growth, but we're not telling a story that brings them all together. Whatever story we are telling doesn't accurately reflect who we are, what we have, and what we do."

A strong narrative is the outwardly facing backbone of a successful organization or brand. It goes beyond telling your origin story, highlighting your latest product, or showcasing your people. A brand narrative is the cohesive and overarching story that ties all your strategic goals, beliefs, and actions into one compelling, repeatable story.

It doesn't just help communicate your purpose. It provides the context of why it's your purpose in the first place. It doesn't just communicate what you do. It articulates the problem that is solved by what you do. And it doesn't assume people believe you. It provides the reasons why they should.

As Scott Svenson, CEO of MOD Pizza, recently pointed out, "Culture travels through stories." Whether it's a tale about a pivotal moment in your company's history or a customer's experience that encapsulates your values, or that time Barb did that thing that made Gary laugh, stories are the threads that weave together the fabric of your culture. They're not just nice-to-haves; they're vital to how your brand is perceived, both internally and externally. And you probably have a million of them. I think you should tell all of them. Repeatedly.

Just remember: If you want to drive growth, you still need a singular, unifying narrative to do it. One narrative that connects purpose and products to drive profit.

Once you have it, it can be sliced and diced, repeated, and reformatted in a multitude of ways, making it versatile across different platforms and audiences.

There are five essential components that every brand narrative should include.

Let's break them down.

1. What's Going On in the World?

Your brand doesn't exist in a vacuum. The first component of your narrative should answer the question: What's going on in the world? Your fundamental beliefs don't come out of thin air. They are in response to the world around you. Whether directly or indirectly, your business is affected by larger trends, societal shifts, and cultural dynamics.

For example, consider the ongoing debate about remote work versus office work. It has created ripple effects that extend far beyond the corporate world. It's impacted everything from home renovations to IT infrastructure, from childcare arrangements to how people book their doctor's appointments. Understanding this context allows you to frame your narrative within a broader conversation, making it more relevant and compelling.

2. What Problem or Opportunity Does That Create?

Once you've identified what's going on in the world, the next step is to pinpoint the problem that arises from it. You don't just want to sell stuff, do you? No. You want to solve a problem that deserves solving. The problem you're trying to solve pulls your purpose from the clouds and down to reality where your customers are.

3. What Do You Believe about That Problem or Opportunity?

This is where your brand's beliefs come into play. Your purpose should be in direct response to the world around you. It's not just about what your product does; it's about why it exists. What do you fundamentally believe about the problem or opportunity you've identified?

Your belief shapes everything you do and helps you connect with your audience on a deeper level. Beyond selling a service, you're aligning with the values and behaviors of the people you want to reach.

4. How Do You Solve That Problem or Pursue That Opportunity?

Now comes the action part of your narrative. What do you do to solve the problem or pursue the opportunity you've identified? This is where your product, service, or unique approach comes into play. It's the tangible aspect of your narrative that shows how you bring your purpose to life.

Your solution should be clear, concise, and directly linked to the problem or opportunity you've outlined.

5. Why Should People Believe You?

Finally, you need to answer the question "Why should people believe you?" A wonderful purpose is useless if people don't believe that you'll actually deliver on it. Let's be honest. Every client interaction has been preceded by a long trail of broken promises, empty offerings, and price points paired with an asterisk and half page of legal copy from other companies. They don't trust institutions. They don't trust government. They don't trust technology. Why the hell should they trust you? People should believe you because of your honesty, transparency, and track record. Whether it's through data, testimonials, or reputation in the industry, you need to provide proof that you're the real deal.

As an example, here's an abbreviated version of our brand narrative for Church+State.

1 **What's going on in the world?** People don't know what's an ad, what's content, and what the difference between the two is.

2 **What problem does that create?** People don't know where to look, and they don't know who to trust.

3 **What do we believe about that problem?** We believe that people used to vote with their wallets, but now they vote with their time.

4 **How do we solve that problem?** We help brands build brand conviction and win the battle for time with employees, customers, and stakeholders.

5 Why should you believe us? We're honest. We're transparent. We're respected. And you can speak to any of our clients, partners, or staff to ask them.

You may not have seen this structure, but you have certainly experienced it. This very book—the one you're holding in your hands—uses the brand narrative structure to tell my story of the purpose of purpose.

1 What's going on in the world? I started the book talking about anti-business sentiments, the lack of empathy shown by leaders, the fact that capitalism isn't working, and the panic that transpired around purpose.

2 What problem does that create? I told you that leaders want to do the right thing, but they don't know what the right thing is because they're not using purpose in the right way.

3 What do I believe about that problem? I believe that leaders need to simplify their actions and focus on driving growth.

4 How should people solve that problem?

a They should articulate and be focused by purpose.

b They should create personalized and frictionless experiences that reinforce their purpose.

c They should communicate what they believe and what they do in compelling and interesting ways so others want to adopt them.

Or, growth comes from what they think, do, and say.

5 **Why should you believe me?** The structure and tone of the book were consciously written with a few things in mind. First, I put purpose before profit. I hope it's clear I'm not pitching you on anything other than my thoughts. I'm not here to sell you something. I'm here to help you. Sure, a book helps drive interest in my other business interests, but I consciously stay away from directly pitching those interests. I hope you get a sense from the tone that it is me writing it—there's no Auto-Tune or ghostwriter involved. This is me typing these words and no one else. I've also backed up my thoughts with personal anecdotes, research, data, and examples from other industries so you can see that the ideas are valid enough to be true across industries outside of mine and yours.

Every speech I give follows this structure.
Every pitch deck we create follows this structure.
Every "About Us" corporate video we create follows this structure.

Once you have your brand narrative, you can (and should) slice and dice it across many uses and many platforms.

A brand narrative isn't just a story—it's the communications heartbeat of your brand, seamlessly connecting your strategy, purpose, and actions into a cohesive and compelling narrative that compels others to join you.

That's growth.

What's your story, morning glory?

THE RUNNER
SAVANNAH BANANAS

ADOPTED THROUGH COMMUNICATIONS

Communicating the Savannah Bananas' purpose and difference was crucial to their success. And it started with the name. After all, if you want to communicate that you're rejecting the status quo, the biggest bang for your branding buck comes from the first point of contact.

They brainstormed a bunch of names, but they were all rather expected—the Savannah Spirits, the Savannah Anchors, the Savannah Ports—direct reflections of the city and traditional baseball names.

Normal names get normal reactions. And normal reactions get normal results. That's the thing with the status quo. It's exactly as good as you expect it will be.

Jesse and the team wanted to be more.

So they held a name-the-team contest, and a 63-year-old nurse, Lynn Moses, submitted "Bananas." Yes. That is *exactly* the type of name that went against the grain and rejected industry norms. But could the name help make an experience that was "better than they ever thought they could be"?

It could, and they knew it right away.

As soon as they saw the name, the ideas came fast and immediate. As Jesse told *Pure Athlete*, "We looked at it and thought yes... 'Go Bananas'; a senior citizen dance team—the Banana Nannas; a male cheerleading team—the Mananas; our mascot, Split; 'Can't stop the peeling,' 'Banana pants'... The ideas just started going."

With that foundation, the Bananas made sure their purpose was reflected in every aspect of their brand's communication strategy.

They create content: They don't have a broadcasting deal with a network to create content for them, so they do it themselves. Unlike traditional baseball teams, the Bananas focus on producing content that is as much about the experience as it is about the game. They create a wide range of content, including behind-the-scenes videos, player skits, and fan interactions, all designed to highlight the fun and unconventional nature of their brand. And they distribute that content directly to the fans, too. The Savannah Bananas have more TikTok followers than every single Major League Baseball team.

They empower fans to spread the word: Who needs ads when your fans are your biggest brand ambassadors? The Bananas have ignored most traditional advertising tactics in favor of a more organic, grassroots approach. Their word-of-mouth marketing approach relies heavily on creating shareable moments and experiences that fans willingly and eagerly spread across their social networks.

They embrace the spotlight: What news outlet wouldn't want a confident and fun guest decked out in a yellow tuxedo and top hat talking about a ridiculously fun and successful business and game? The Bananas' willingness to embrace the spotlight and share their story has earned them widespread media coverage, including in this book(!).

They connect the personal brand to the corporate brand: Jesse Cole has used every platform available to share the team's story, from social media to community events, ensuring that everyone knows what the Bananas stand for.

His personal brand as an enlightened and fun entrepreneur—always appearing in his yellow tuxedo—has become synonymous with the team's quirky and innovative approach. He's done podcasts, keynotes, appearances, and more. His story is the Bananas story. And for every person who's interested in the baseball experience, there's another one who is interested in the business experience.

Their communication, much like their baseball, is a bold and brilliant spectacle, ensuring that the world would never look at a banana—or a ballpark—the same way again.

"Google it."

CONFUCIUS

GO
FORTH
AND
MULTIPLY

Don't look for shortcuts. Just do the work.

Vroom Vroom

I failed my driving test when I was 16.

There, I said it.

My brother's car broke down on test day, and my good friend Mike Watson stepped in and kindly let me borrow his tinted Chevy Malibu. Halfway through the test, the examiner started freaking out. She was yelling at the top of her lungs. "Pull over! Pull over! You're breaking the law!"

Me? What was she talking about?

As I pulled to the side and the examiner composed herself, she said that she was failing me on the spot for my reckless and irresponsible behavior. Apparently, I was speeding. What?? No way.

I was only going... Oh no. I looked down and realized right then that Mike's speedometer was in *miles* per hour, not *kilometers*. I wasn't going 50 kilometers per hour down a residential street. I was going *50 miles per hour* down a residential street. With children. And crossing guards. And signs that said "Slow down, idiot. Kids are playing."

Don't worry, I eventually passed and got my license, but I've always had a bit of a heavy foot. I should have been a race car driver, but I never had the will or interest to learn or the access to a Ferrari to practice. So I don't know much about racing—but what I *do* know should interest you.

I doesn't matter if it's F1, NASCAR, or any other type of race, here's what I know. Car races are won in two places: They're won in the pits, and they're won in the corners.

Winning in the pits is all about teamwork. You need a group of people who have been recruited because of an area of specialty. They have been trained to be the best at what they do when you most need them to do it. Beyond that, they need to be inspired to do it, they need to be informed to do it, and they need to be empowered to do it. The team needs to work together with maximum efficiency—everyone focused on their tasks in a beautifully choreographed sequence to get the car back on the track in record time.

Races are also won in the corners.

The straightaways might look flashy, but they're easy. You put the pedal to the metal, lock your elbows, and gun it. Whoever built the best machine six months before the race will win in the straightaways.

But races are never won in the straightaways.

See, the corners are where the pros show up. This is where talent comes in. This is where experience and confidence and know-how and guts and daring and ability all contribute to a driver being able to beat everyone else on the track.

When a driver enters a corner out of the straightaway, the first thing they do is slow the car down. They need to slow the car down to gain control of it so it doesn't skid off the track. They have to go from a state of chaos entering the corner to a state of composure *in* the corner.

They take a deep breath and know they're in control. But once they hit that state of composure, the driver has to ensure they don't enter a state of complacency. They can't chill out in the corner. They can't lose their focus in the corner. They can't take their eyes off the road in the corner. And they can't sit back and wait for the next straightaway in the corner.

Races are won by drivers who accelerate in the middle of the corner.

You accelerate in the middle of the corner so that when you leave the corner, you do so with great momentum. Do it and you get to lap everyone who hesitated.

In our careers and in our business, we all have corners.

Maybe it's a downturn in the economy. Or it's a slow sales stretch. Or seasonality in your category. Or a geopolitical crisis or a damaged supply chain or a million other possible things. If you need growth because of the state of the world around you, you need to ensure you don't enter a state of complacency, throw your hands up, and say, "What are you gonna do?" You can't wait it out. You need to accelerate in the corner.

Because if you don't, guess what? You're resigned.

You're resigned to waiting it out. You're resigned to letting the world dictate your place. You're resigned to letting growth happen instead of consciously and proactively trying to make growth begin.

Growth is not a nice-to-have, it's a need-to-have.

The race doesn't end.
We're always driving.
We're always turning.
We're always accelerating.
We're always braking.
We're always handling corners.

Would you rather look at the exhaust pipe of somebody in front of you and be constantly forced to react to their actions, or would you prefer to be out in front with the open road ahead of you?

It's time to accelerate. Let's go. Let's grow.

THE RUNNER
SAVANNAH BANANAS

DO BANANAS GROW?
THE SUCCESS OF THE SAVANNAH BANANAS

Why be clever when I can be blunt?

The Savannah Bananas' waitlist for tickets is close to two million people long.

TWO MILLION PEOPLE ARE WAITING FOR THE CHANCE TO EXPERIENCE BANANA BALL.

The 2023 Banana Ball World Tour was 100 percent sold out and generated an estimated $10 million in ticket sales alone.

In 2024, the Bananas and their partner touring teams played to sold-out crowds at six Major League Baseball ballparks: Fenway Park in Boston, Minute Maid Park in Houston, Nationals Park in DC, LoanDepot Park in Miami, Citizens Bank Park in Philadelphia, and Progressive Field in Cleveland.

They've been featured in national media, and their unique approach to baseball has inspired other teams and businesses to rethink their models. Financially, they have turned a struggling team into a thriving business, proving that a purpose-driven approach focused on creating exceptional experiences can lead to extraordinary growth.

Their fans aren't just there to see a game. They're there to experience it, engage in it, and—as ambassadors—share it. Bananas' merch flies off the shelves, their content continues to go viral, and their progressive approach to rethinking business is more popular than tired cases like Zappos and Netflix.

The Savannah Bananas have shown that with the right purpose, focused execution, and a commitment to removing friction, it's possible to turn even the most traditional and stagnant industries into dynamic, growing enterprises.

The Bananas went beyond revitalizing baseball in Savannah; they created a cultural phenomenon that challenged the status quo and inspired a new generation of fans.

And it all started because Jesse Cole wanted to grow personally. His growth led to team growth. The team growth led to the growth of operations, HR, sponsorship, ticketing, sales, and more. The systems growth led to organizational growth. Organizational growth led to the growth of an entirely new industry. And when all those things grow, the community that they're a part of grows.

Thanks to Jesse Cole, Bananas grow in Savannah, Georgia.

Grab Your Buns

When my good friend Sarah Wells was training for (and competing in) the Olympics, she would put her hair in a *really* tight bun so, in her words, "not even a speck of hair could flop in the wind and slow me down."

When an elite athlete gets close to the Olympic level of competition, they don't look to knock minutes or seconds off their time. They deploy specific techniques to take milliseconds off their time. Fractions of fractions of seconds. Sarah's personal best time on the 400-meter hurdles is 55.65 seconds. *Not* 55.66.

They change the fabric in their uniform.

They position their thumbs a certain way.

They decrease the number of times they blink.

Heck, some even deploy the Wellsian Bun Strategy to help them get faster, higher, stronger. (Citius, Altius, Fortius!)

That works for Sarah, and it works for other Olympians. But if I entered the 400-meter hurdles, it wouldn't work for me.

The problem with so much business advice given by a new wave of socially deployed (ahem) "thought leaders" is that they preach their little tips without ever acknowledging that without base talent, the tricks and hacks are useless. There's a reason they're called "tricks"—the only person you're tricking is yourself.

If your best 400-meter hurdles time is over three minutes, it doesn't matter how tight your bun is.

And if your growth strategy is built around companies promising leads, repeated cold calling, trying to buy credibility, or any number of other "growth hacks," it doesn't matter how good your CRM system is. Your growth is going to suck.

Don't fall for tips and tricks.
Don't look for shortcuts.
Don't try to game the system.
Just do the work.

This Is the Test

Earlier, I mentioned the stress of the first few days and weeks of the pandemic as I found myself with a second beautiful child but with a loss of speaking revenue and an unclear path forward for our people, our clients, and our business.

In chapter 3, I said, "I invested in personal growth. I knew that I needed a way to inspire and inform people from the comfort of my own house. So, I did."

If only it was that easy. The reality? I was in a horrible place (as many were). I was totally resigned to waiting it out while simultaneously thinking I would lose it all before the pandemic ended.

And then my friend Peter Katz showed up.

It was midnight. I was up. Everyone else was asleep. It was quiet. I was in my office watching random low-calorie content whose only value was wasting time.

And then a video from Peter entered my feed.

Peter is an accomplished musician, speaker, and an absolutely wonderful human being. Consistent with his generous nature, Peter created a video teaching other musicians how to do virtual concerts. He showed them how they could kick-start their COVID music career in this new virtual environment; he demonstrated what software to use, how to set up their microphones, where to put their cameras, and how to play their instruments to a virtual audience.

I play campfire guitar—you know, all songs featuring G, C, and D—but I'm not a musician. Still, I was incredibly inspired by both the information presented and the humanity that Peter showed to help his fellow musicians figure it out.

It was the kick in the ass I needed. Here was Peter being totally selfless. He embraced the limitations imposed upon him and invested in his own personal growth, while taking the time to help other people realize theirs.

Immediately after the video ended, I wrote down, "We're all students right now."

I thought that was the positive spin that I needed in that weird time. And I thought that while Peter had stood up for musicians, someone needed to stand up for the basic concept of learning. Someone needed to get beyond the "These are unprecedented times" bullshit that ruled our airwaves and actually inspire someone to do something.

Yes. These were unprecedented times. Now what?

At the time, one of our clients was Centennial College, a large postsecondary institution in Canada. I thought they could and should stand up for learning. I wanted them to be the ones to do it.

So right then and there at about 12:15 a.m., I wrote a script inspired by my line that was inspired by Peter. My only thought around the script was "What would a professor say to their students right now?"

I finished it in 10 minutes.

And the spot we would eventually shoot was that script essentially unchanged.

Growth isn't a destination—it's a mindset.

This is what I wrote that night:

Well, I bet you didn't think school was going to be like this, did you?

Don't worry. You're not alone.

We're all learning new ways of working, parenting, eating, shopping.

Athletes are learning new ways to train.

Musicians are learning new ways to play.

Nurses are learning new ways to heal.

Restaurants are learning new ways to serve.

Even teachers like me are learning new ways to teach.

Every single one of us is learning new ways of living and being and doing.

You are. Yeah, you are.

Sure, it's a challenge, but it's also an opportunity.

Class is in session.

Don't be late.

Sit in the front row.

Show up ready to learn.

Eager to learn.

Yearning to learn something new.

> Because the difference between simply being in this moment and thriving in this moment is what we learn from this moment.
>
> And no, this won't be on the test.
> This *is* the test.

The agency owner in me obviously said that this script was written for our valued client. We always put our clients first.

Much later, though, I realized that it was written for me.

I needed a spark to start my own growth. My growth could hopefully inspire our team to grow. And when our team grows, our clients grow. When our clients grow, our business grows.

Our agency saw "unprecedented" growth over the pandemic, and we've continued that trajectory. All of it started with a video for helping musicians play to a live audience when it seemed impossible to do so.

It sparked my growth.
I hope this book, in some small way, sparks yours.
Let's go. Let's grow.

Acknowledgments

I WRITE A LOT. For those who follow me on LinkedIn, you know that I usually share two to three posts a day. Some of those are just me thinking out loud, open-mic style. Other posts are my responses to specific articles, posts, or think pieces written by others that inform me. Or inspire me. Or challenge me. Or frustrate me. Or direct me. So I write. And I post. And then you respond. Your comments help crystallize my thoughts. They point out when I'm wrong, when I'm right, or when I need to go back and rethink what I thought.

From LinkedIn, I polish my thoughts and take them to the stage so I can test them in speeches before live audiences from a variety of industries around the world. I kill some of those thoughts, keep some, extend some, and minimize some. A nugget becomes a bit, and a bit becomes a bucket, and a bucket becomes a chapter, and chapters become a book.

I want to acknowledge every single person who follows along and is engaged in my process. If you're a connection or follower who likes, comments, or shares. If you're an event planner who has put me before your teams or clients. If you're an audience member who has applauded or booed. If you're someone who writes or rants or asks or solves. We're all in this together. This book doesn't happen without you.

James Harbeck, your wonderful editorial guidance was *exactly* what this book needed (not to mention the writer). And to Jesse, Trena, Peter, Rony, Felicia, and the rest of the team at Page Two, thanks for the tremendous advice, support, and patience. Deadline? *What deadline?*

To my business partners, Robin, Natalie, and Guillaume, and to the Group 219 teams at Church+State, Airfoil, and Substance, thanks for your brilliance and dedication to doing the right things for the best people working with the best clients.

To Martin, Farah, Paula, Mélanie, and the whole Speakers Spotlight team, thanks for continuing to shine that spotlight in my direction. I can't believe we've been partners for 17 years. Incredible. Here's to the next 17!

To Scott Stratten. Texting from the road to share stories, scores, and laughs will always brighten my day. *Go Vegas! Go Lions! Go Jays!*

To Jason Thompson. Of all the wonderful stories you craft and help craft, our lifelong friendship is still my favorite. Thanks for the many important Mountain Minutes.

To Mitch Joel. From stand-up bits to important career advice to setting up this book with such brilliance in the foreword, thanks for continuing to share with generosity. Next MTL breakfast is on me.

And to Christy, Max, and Benny. You're sitting beside me on a plane as I write this. You bring me more joy and love than any one person could ever imagine. You make me smile. You make me laugh. You make me cry. Here's to tears of joy. I love you.

References

BP. "Our Purpose." bp.com/en/global/corporate/who-we-are/our-purpose.html.

Bridesmaid for Hire. "About." bridesmaidforhire.com/about.

Brockman, Charles. "Fan Looks to Sue Whitecaps over Lionel Messi's No-Show." Sportsnet, June 6, 2024. sportsnet.ca/mls/article/fan-looks-to-sue-whitecaps-over-lionel-messis-no-show.

Brouillet, Jerome (@jeromebrouilletphotography). "Touched by grace..." Instagram post, July 30, 2024. instagram.com/jeromebrouilletphotography/p/C-Dq2nYvnmZ.

Burnham, Bo, dir. *Bo Burnham: Inside*. 2021. Netflix. Film, 87 min.

Burnham, Bo, and Chris Storer, dirs. *Bo Burnham: Make Happy*. 2016. Netflix. Film, 60 min.

Canada's Walk of Fame. "Russell Peters." canadaswalkoffame.com/inductee/russell-peters.

Coca-Cola Freestyle. coca-colafreestyle.com.

Coke Solutions. "Coca-Cola Freestyle." cokesolutions.com/equipment/coca-cola-freestyle.

Cole, Jesse (@yellowtuxjesse). "How the Savannah Bananas Hire." TikTok, May 28, 2024. tiktok.com/@yellowtuxjesse/video/7374207437034900782.

Cole, Jesse (@yellowtuxjesse). "If you are obsessed with the metrics..." TikTok, June 20, 2024. tiktok.com/@yellowtuxjesse/video/7382714777757322539.

Creative Salon. "Have We Reached Peak Purpose?" December 15, 2022. creative.salon/articles/features/qotw-peak-purpose.

Da Costa, Cassie, and Chris Murphy. "What Is Bo Burnham's *Inside* Really Trying to Say?" *Vanity Fair*, June 10, 2021. vanityfair.com/hollywood/2021/06/what-is-bo-burnhams-inside-really-trying-to-say.

ESPN. "How the Savannah Bananas Have Become the Greatest Show in Baseball." *SportsCenter*, August 22, 2021. YouTube video. youtube.com/watch?v=T5RkB7_qNh8.

Estis, Ryan. "Make Baseball Fun and Put Fans First." RyanEstis.com, May 17, 2022. ryanestis.com/make-baseball-fun-and-put-fans-first.

Expansive. "Hybrid Offices: Creating Space for How Employees Want to Work." expansive.com/your-guide-to-the-hybrid-office-space-model.

Fern, Ong Sor. "Instagram Sensation Museum of Ice Cream Opens in S'pore with Sprinkle Pool, Disco and More." *Straits Times*, August 19, 2021. straitstimes.com/life/arts/singapore-gets-a-taste-of-the-museum-of-ice-cream.

Fox, Jesse David, host. *Good One: A Podcast about Jokes*, season 3, episode 7, "Bo Burnham's Can't Handle This." Vulture, July 2, 2018.

Franz, Annette. "Unexpected Experiences: Disrupting the Moving Industry." CX Journey, May 10, 2023. cx-journey.com/2023/05/unexpected-experiences-disrupting-the-moving-industry.html.

Gartner. "Gartner CEO Survey Finds Growth Is the Top Business Priority for 2024, Reaching Highest Level in 10 Years." Press release, May 22, 2024. gartner.com/en/newsroom/press-releases/2024-05-22-gartner-ceo-survey-finds-growth-is-the-top-business-priority-for-2024--reaching-highest-level-in-10-years.

Gelles, David. *The Man Who Broke Capitalism: How Jack Welch Gutted the Heartland and Crushed the Soul of Corporate America—and How to Undo His Legacy*. Simon & Schuster, 2022.

"GM's Path to an All-Electric Future | CES 2021." GMC Hummer EV, February 11, 2021. YouTube video. youtube.com/watch?v=wjVDKH4KeOo.

Godin, Seth. "Choosing Your Problems." *Seth's Blog*, March 4, 2023. seths.blog/2023/03/choosing-your-problems.

Goldsmith, Kelly, and Marshall Goldsmith. "You Can Be More." *Chief Executive.* chiefexecutive.net/kelly-marshall-goldsmith-you-can-be-more.

Goler, Lori, Janelle Gale, Brynn Harrington, and Adam Grant. "The 3 Things Employees Really Want: Career, Community, Cause." *Harvard Business Review*, February 20, 2018. hbr.org/2018/02/people-want-3-things-from-work-but-most-companies-are-built-around-only-one.

Google. "Google's Disability Alliance." careers.google.com/stories/googles-disability-alliance.

Hannam, Lisa. "What's Russell Peters Doing Now? Investing, and It's a Laugh." *MoneySense*, July 15, 2022. moneysense.ca/save/investing/russell-peters.

Harter, Jim. "4 Factors Driving Record-High Employee Engagement in U.S." Gallup Workplace, February 4, 2020. gallup.com/workplace/284180/employees-need-most-right.aspx.

Herold, Kristi. "In the last 28 years of leading JAM..." LinkedIn, September 2024. linkedin.com/posts/kristi-herold_networking-socialsports-community-activity-7237095815037493248-exBX.

Hicks, Katie. "How Mattel Gave the Barbie Brand a Makeover." *Marketing Brew*, October 18, 2023. marketingbrew.com/stories/2023/10/18/how-mattel-gave-the-barbie-brand-a-makeover.

Improper. "Have We Reached Peak Purpose? We've Barely Started." Little Black Book, October 5, 2023. lbbonline.com/news/have-we-reached-peak-purpose-weve-barely-started.

INSEAD Knowledge and Mark Mortensen. "How to Work Out What Your Employees Really Want." INSEAD Knowledge, January 17, 2023. knowledge.insead.edu/career/how-work-out-what-your-employees-really-want.

Isidore, Chris, and Matt Egan. "The Dismantling of GE, Once America's Iconic 'Everything Company,' Is Now Complete." *CNN Business*, April 2, 2024. cnn.com/2024/04/02/business/general-electric-split-explained/index.html.

JohnWallStreet. "Savannah Bananas Eye 500% Revenue Increase with '23 Roadshow." Sportico, November 1, 2022. sportico.com/business/commerce/2022/savannah-bananas-eye-500-1234692265.

"Jon Stewart Smashes the Myth of Corporate Morality in Pride, BLM, and Beyond." *The Daily Show*, June 10, 2024. YouTube video. youtu.be/TWVbzOWQ3s8?si=x2uNs_oE-Mzb7pKv.

Klinghoffer, Dawn, and Elizabeth McCune. "Why Microsoft Measures Employee Thriving, Not Engagement." *Harvard Business Review*, June 24, 2022. hbr.org/2022/06/why-microsoft-measures-employee-thriving-not-engagement.

L'Oréal Paris. "Skin Genius." lorealparisusa.com/skin-genius-landing-page.

Le, Vanna. "The Top-Earning Comedians of 2013: No. 3 Russell Peters." *Forbes*, July 11, 2013. forbes.com/pictures/eimi45ldg/no-3-russell-peters/#gallerycontent.

Liebenson, Donald. "How Steve Martin and Illustrator Harry Bliss Ended Up Working on the 'Upbeat Book' We All Need Right Now." *The Washington Post*, November 16, 2020. washingtonpost.com/entertainment/books/steve-martin-wealth-of-pigeons/2020/11/14/303fb986-25e3-11eb-a688-5298ad5d580a_story.html.

Lund, Susan, Anu Madgavkar, James Manyika, Sven Smit, Kweilin Ellingrud, Mary Meaney, and Olivia Robinson. *The Future of Work after COVID-19*. McKinsey Global Institute, February 18, 2021. mckinsey.com/featured-insights/future-of-work/the-future-of-work-after-covid-19.

Mandell, Jon. "When Designing Customer Experiences, Don't Confuse Speed with Ease." *Adweek*, March 3, 2023. adweek.com/commerce/designing-customer-experiences.

MarketScale. "The Savannah Bananas: Winning with Fans First." marketscale.com/industries/original-series/the-savannah-bananas/fans-first.

Markham, Glen. "Should I Stay or Should I Go? The Hard Uncertain Choice." LinkedIn, June 29, 2021. linkedin.com/posts/glenmarkham_should-i-stay-or-should-i-go-the-hard-uncertain-activity-6815629828637782016-0gwJ.

Martin, Roger. "A Strategic Framework for Growth." Medium, July 22, 2024. rogermartin.medium.com/a-strategic-framework-for-growth-5772d43fe93d.

Martin, Roger L. *Fixing the Game: Bubbles, Crashes, and What Capitalism Can Learn from the NFL*. Harvard Business Review Press, 2011.

Mattel. "The Dream Gap Project." shop.mattel.com/en-ca/pages/barbie-dream-gap.

Mayoquín, Orlando. "In Latest Stunt, Airbnb Lists the 'Up' House. It Floats." *New York Times*, May 1, 2024. nytimes.com/2024/05/01/business/airbnb-up-house-shrek-listings.html.

McKinsey Global Institute. "At a Glance." In *The Future of Wealth and Growth Hangs in the Balance*. May 24, 2023. mckinsey.com/mgi/overview/the-future-of-wealth-and-growth-hangs-in-the-balance#at-a-glance.

Michal. "A Tour of Google's Cool New Mountain View Office." OfficeLovin', March 2020. officelovin.com/2020/03/a-tour-of-googles-cool-new-mountain-view-office.

Migdon, Brooke. "*Sports Illustrated* Swimsuit Launches Initiative to Only Advertise Companies 'Creating Change for Women.'" *Changing America*, February 7, 2022. thehill.com/changing-america/respect/diversity-inclusion/593167-sports-illustrated-swimsuit-launches-initiative.

Moversville Connect. "Cleaning Success to Moving Revolution: Ron's Remarkable Journey Founding Pink Zebra Moving Franchise." *Moving Company Owners Podcast*. connect.moversville.com/cleaning-success-to-moving-revolution-rons-remarkable-journey-founding-pink-zebra-moving-franchise.

Museum of Ice Cream. "Pick Your Location." museumoficecream.com.

Myers, Brittney. "Mastercard True Name: Complete Guide." Motley Fool Money, November 18, 2024. fool.com/the-ascent/credit-cards/mastercard-true-name.

Nixon, Sam. "Going Bananas: The Economic Home Run Scored by the Savannah Bananas." PicksWise, May 30, 2023. pickswise.com/mlb/savannah-bananas-earnings.

Notable Life. "5 Things You Should Know about Russell Peters." notablelife.com/5-things-you-should-know-about-russell-peters.

Pedorthic Association of Canada. "What Is a Pedorthist? The Role of a Pedorthist." pedorthic.ca/insurance-providers/the-role-of-a-pedorthist.

Petriglieri, Gianpiero. "Driving Organizational Change—without Abandoning Tradition." *Harvard Business Review*, April 24, 2023. hbr.org/2023/04/driving-organizational-change-without-abandoning-tradition.

Philip Morris International. "PMI's Statement of Purpose." pmi.com/statement-of-purpose.

Pink Zebra Moving. "About Us." pinkzebramoving.com.

Pure Athlete. "Savannah Bananas Founder Jesse Cole." *The Pure Athlete Podcast*, March 27, 2024. YouTube video. youtube.com/watch?v=HaN2jbkIbUQ.

Rudy, Katie. "Lessons from Leaders: How Jesse Cole and the Savannah Bananas Create the 'Greatest Show Possible.'" EngageMint, June 14, 2022. engagemintpartners.com/lessons-from-leaders-create-the-greatest-show-jesse-cole.

Salesforce. "Salesforce Tower: San Francisco's Newest Landmark." salesforcetower.com.

Satell, Greg. "Why GE's Incredible Turnaround Could Be a Sign of the Times." *Digital Tonto*, February 18, 2024. digitaltonto.com/2024/is-whats-good-for-general-electric-good-for-america.

Savannah Bananas. "About Us." thesavannahbananas.com/about_us.

Strategy staff. "Have We Reached Peak Purpose?" *Strategy*, March 19, 2024. strategyonline.ca/2024/03/19/have-we-reached-peak-purpose.

Sularia, Sanjeev. "How Shopify Is Shifting the E-Commerce Landscape." *Forbes*, January 22, 2021. forbes.com/sites/forbestechcouncil/2021/01/22/how-shopify-is-shifting-the-e-commerce-landscape.

Suzman, James. *Work: A Deep History, from the Stone Age to the Age of Robots*. Penguin, 2021.

Tabrizi, Behnam. "How Microsoft Became Innovative Again." *Harvard Business Review*, February 20, 2023. hbr.org/2023/02/how-microsoft-became-innovative-again.

Tulfo, Erika. "Netflix to Open 2 Massive Venues with Experiences, Shops Themed to Its Shows." *CNN Business*, June 18, 2024. cnn.com/2024/06/18/business/netflix-house-locations-experiential-venues/index.html.

Turner, Corey. "Banana Ball—The Business Behind the Savannah Bananas." LinkedIn, May 4, 2022. linkedin.com/pulse/banana-ball-business-behind-savannah-bananas-corey-turner.

Valdes-Dapena, Peter. "GM Redesigns Its Logo after More Than 50 Years." *CNN Business*, January 8, 2021. cnn.com/2021/01/08/cars/new-gm-logo/index.html.

Valerio, Pablo. "Google: IoT Can Help the Disabled." *Information Week*, March 10, 2015. informationweek.com/it-leadership/google-iot-can-help-the-disabled.

Webster, Peter. "Google's Mountain View, California Campus Is a Biophilic Haven." *Interior Design*, January 24, 2024. interiordesign.net/projects/google-mountain-view-california-campus.

Wheless, Erika. "Sonic's CMO on Its New Campaign, Changing Media Approach and Why It Stuck with Mother." *Ad Age*, June 3, 2024. adage.com/article/marketing-news-strategy/sonic-cmo-new-ads-consumer-prices-media-and-agency-mother/2563116.

Williams, Evan. "GM Logo Gets Overhauled: Here's a Look Back at the Old Ones." *Auto Trader*, January 11, 2021. autotrader.ca/editorial/20210111/gm-logo-gets-overhauled-here-s-a-look-back-at-the-old-ones.

Winkie, Luke. "Odd Job: 'Professional Bridesmaid' Is an Actual Job. Meet a Woman Who Does It." *Vox*, December 6, 2019. vox.com/the-goods/2019/12/6/20981896/professional-bridesmaid-job.

PHOTO: TONY EDGAR

About the Author

Founder of marketing agency Church+State and host and executive producer of the podcast *The Coup*, Ron Tite has been an award-winning creative director for some of the world's most respected brands. He coauthored *Everyone's an Artist (or at Least They Should Be)*, wrote *Think Do Say*, wrote and produced the stage play *The Canadian Baby Bonus*, has written for television, penned a children's book, and hosted the award-winning comedy show Monkey Toast. Ron speaks on creativity, innovation, and corporate strategy to leading organizations all over the world.

thinkdosay.com · rontite.com · @rontite · churchstate.co

FROM WORDS TO WORK

THIS MAY BE the end of the book, but it could also be the start of your TDS journey. And if you think that sounds like a spiritual quote from a dead philosopher, you're probably right. Regardless, if you want to dive deeper into the purpose of purpose, there are a bunch of options.

LINK DO SAY

I'm really active on LinkedIn and share updates, resources, content, and reports a few times a day. Come on over and follow along. There's only one caveat: no pitch slapping.

THINK DO SAY MORE

To explore a variety of resources, go to **thinkdosay.com**.

THINK DO HAVE ME SAY

I speak all over the world for organizations and associations from all industries and sectors. To explore options, go to **rontite.com** or directly to Speakers Spotlight at **speakers.ca/speakers/ron-tite**.

SAY WHAT YOU THINK

I hate asking people, "Can you give the book an online review?" Hate it. So I won't ask. But you know . . . it helps.